D0126770

¡HOLA PAPI!

How to Come Out in a Walmart Parking Lot

and Other Life Lessons

JOHN PAUL BRAMMER

SIMON & SCHUSTER

NEW YORK   LONDON   TORONTO   SYDNEY   NEW DELHI

Simon & Schuster
1230 Avenue of the Americas
New York, NY 10020

First Simon & Schuster hardcover edition June 2021

SIMON & SCHUSTER and colophon are registered
trademarks of Simon & Schuster, Inc.

For information about special discounts for bulk purchases,
please contact Simon & Schuster Special Sales at 1-866-506-1949
or business@simonandschuster.com.

The Simon & Schuster Speakers Bureau can bring authors
to your live event. For more information or to book an event,
contact the Simon & Schuster Speakers Bureau at 1-866-248-3049
or visit our website at www.simonspeakers.com.

Interior design by Michelle Marchese

Manufactured in the United States of America

1   3   5   7   9   10   8   6   4   2

Library of Congress Cataloging-in-Publication Data has been applied for.

ISBN 978-1-9821-4149-3
ISBN 978-1-9821-4152-3 (ebook)

For Madre

Essays

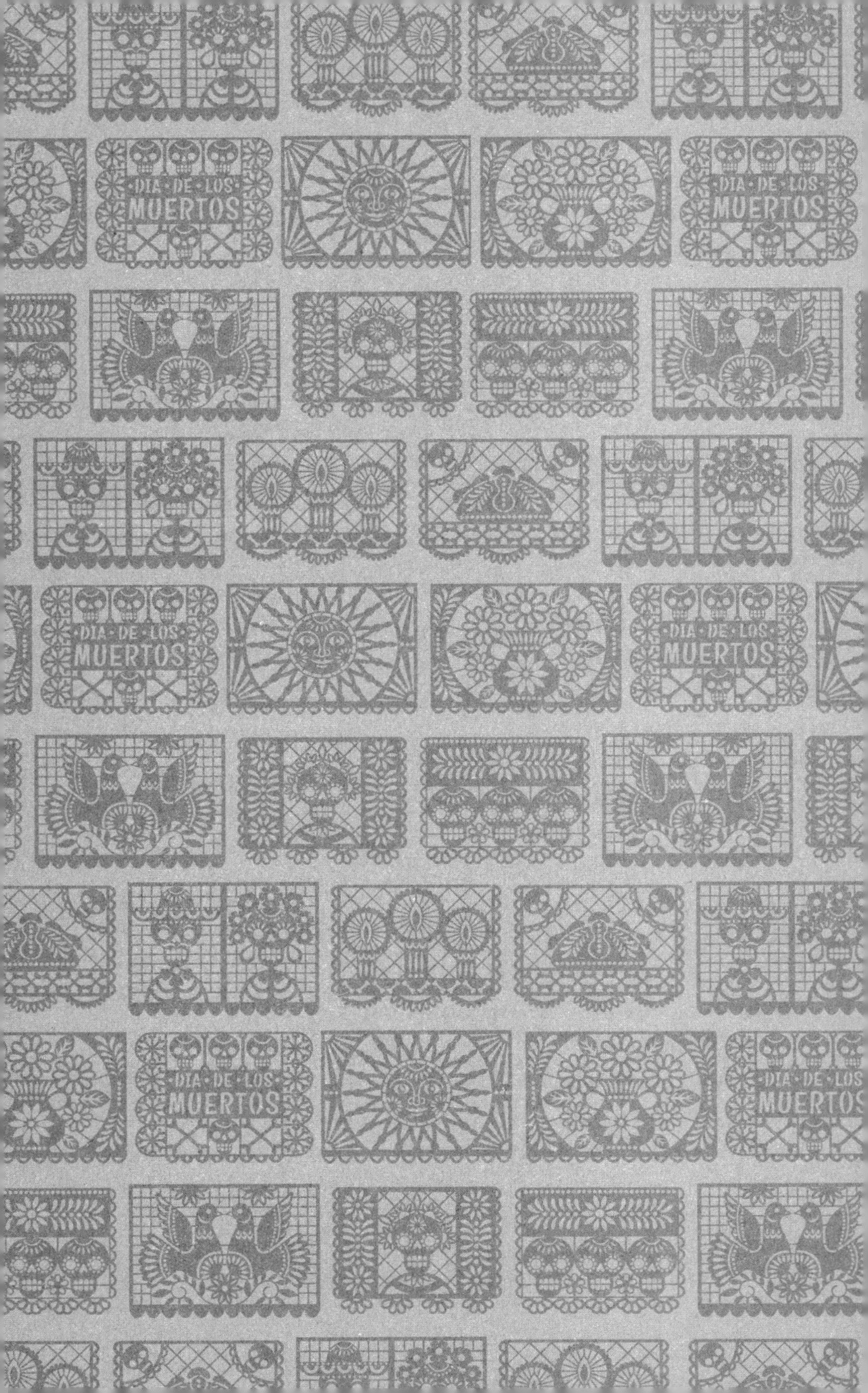
DIA DE LOS
MUERTOS

Author's Note

¡Hola amigos!

While the following stories recount my lived experiences, many of the characters have had their names and identifying details shifted or have been rendered as composite characters. That's when a few different people are put in a blender and turned into one person. Some dialogue has also been re-created from memory.

¡Hola Papi!

Are you even qualified to help me?

Signed,
Reader

How to Answer a Letter, Part 1

I was warned not to download Grindr. I remember the conversation clearly. I was a junior in college at the time. It was a sun-drenched afternoon in 2011, and I was sitting on a bench with a Swedish guy named Erik whom I'd met off a sleazy hookup site called Adam4Adam with a nigh-unusable interface. Erik, a senior, had taken it upon himself to show me the ropes of gay life for reasons I'd naïvely assumed were platonic. I was twenty years old and had only been out of the closet for a couple of months.

"Oh goodness," he said, his regular preamble to addressing my mistakes—my not knowing what a "top" or "bottom" was, the menagerie of mediocre men I'd arranged to have sex with, none of which ever met Erik's standards. "You haven't heard of Grindr?"

Erik was manifestly chlorinated: an avid swimmer, he had bleach-blond hair and matching bleach-white skin. He always smelled clean in a chemical way, always seemed like he'd rather be swimming; he'd make absent paddling motions with his hands while walking. He'd drag me to the pool to criticize my form and show me what a real breaststroke should look like (mine was a "stroke" in the loosest sense of the word).

And I went, Reader. I went because I was desperate for the knowledge Erik held so casually: how to date and hook up and live as a gay person, things I didn't yet know how to do. I'd grown up in the Oklahoma countryside, where my only real exposure to gayness had been through the judges on *America's Next Top Model* and an estranged uncle on the white side of the family who was too busy chain-smoking and drinking Franzia out of a box to make idle chitchat.

I worried, Reader, that I had gotten too late a start on this "being gay" business. I was an all-or-nothing kind of person. I wasn't gay until one day when I decided that, no, actually, I was. Aside from one failed romantic endeavor with my best friend from high school, I hadn't really fooled around with guys while I was in the closet. I didn't watch gay porn or hit up gay bars only to go back to pretending I was straight. But once I'd committed to "being gay," I immediately started throwing myself at whoever would have me, which at least brought a colorful new cast of characters into my life, Erik's pallor notwithstanding.

"What exactly is Grindr?" I asked.

"It's nothing a sweet girl like you needs to know about," Erik said, chewing his gum and staring off into the middle distance. Erik always seemed like he had something better to do than muck about with me, which made it all the more confusing that he kept inviting me places. "Stay away from it. You'll thank me later."

"It's a hookup app?" I said, pressing him. At the time, during my personal Stone Age, the only apps I had on my phone were

Candy Crush and Facebook, like a soccer mom in the suburbs. My scandalous homosexual activities were reserved for my laptop during the witching hour, when I would log in to Adam4Adam and exchange nudes with faceless strangers, seeking the dopamine rush of approval. The notion that I could get such a thing on my smartphone was novel and exciting.

"It's *the* gay hookup app," Erik said, as if I were the world's purest baby. "But for, like, the worst people. Dylan is always on it. Have you met Dylan? Oh, you will." Erik was always threatening me with these inevitable landmarks of my journey, prophecies of dates gone awry and conflicts with catty gossips whom Erik always referred to as "she" and "her," which only confused me further. "She'll find you," he said. "Don't worry. She'll get to you."

The first thing I did after freeing myself from Erik for the day was, of course, to download Grindr.

I opened it up in my apartment, an orange icon with an ominous black mask on it (the color scheme was inverted back then). I was introduced to "the grid": row upon row of profiles—men, all within reach, mere feet away. The guys I'd glanced at in coffee shops. The men I'd checked out at the gym. The classmates who made me wonder, *What if?* All made tangible with a little blue chat button.

I was instantly hooked.

It was on this app that, for the first time ever, some white guy greeted me by saying, "Hola papi." I'd never really considered myself any kind of "papi." I was a mixed-race Mexican American with noodle arms who couldn't legally drink yet. But in the overwhelming influx of everything that came with coming out—new customs, new vocabulary, new ways of seeing myself—I didn't think too much of it. I accepted it as another sideways fact of my chaotic new life and moved on.

In that long process of moving on, Grindr and I stayed together, even as Erik faded into my past. When I took an internship with the Austin Film Festival for a summer before my senior year of college, Grindr went with me. When I studied abroad in Barcelona, I'd hang out in cafés with Wi-Fi and open Grindr. When I moved to DC for a blogging job, and then to New York for another gig, "the grid" was a constant in my life. The men came and went, with varying degrees of success. But Grindr was forever.

I wouldn't have called myself a sex addict, Reader. I wasn't having near enough sex to qualify for that. I was more of an affirmation junkie. I was into the idea of being wanted by people who didn't have any obligation to want me. After a life spent languishing with repressed desires, it felt good to openly want and be wanted. To lust, to flirt, to show off and to be shown—even if nothing came of it—was a destination unto itself. On the grid, I got to sit and survey all my options, my delicious options, exquisitely illustrated possibilities, at no cost. I developed a visceral, Pavlovian reaction to the *brrrrp* of a new message.

After logging countless hours—years!—on the foul application, it was in 2017 that I was beamed up to the mother ship of Grindr HQ in Los Angeles. It seemed like the natural conclusion of our journey together, but it was only the beginning.

A friend I'd met in the New York gay Latino hive mind had recently been hired as a staff writer for a new editorial brand published by Grindr, called INTO (a clever play on the common Grindr refrain "What are you into?," the phrase most asked by gay men sniffing out possible hookups). My friend Mathew Rodriguez asked if I'd be interested in pitching a regular column for INTO. At the time, I was working as an associate producer at NBC News, commuting daily to 30 Rock and crying on the M train while composing *Teen Vogue* articles on my phone's notes app about Kylie Jenner's being spotted with a fidget spinner. I'd get to work, report on the day's atrocities for NBC, rinse, and then repeat.

So, really, what did I have to lose?

In fact, I had everything to gain. Ever in the freelance mindset of "you are going to fail and bring shame to your family unless you say yes to everything," I said yes and tried to engineer a weekly column for weekly checks. The problem was, I didn't trust myself to come up with a new topic to write about with such frequency. I would need an inexhaustible well of material.

An advice column was the perfect solution: readers would supply me with a weekly topic, and I could tap into the infinitely renewable resource of gay drama to fuel it. A triumph for the young man who once sat on a park bench with a Swedish swimmer, feeling he'd missed the boat on "being gay." I'm pretty sure Erik was Swedish, anyway.

In the tradition of clever app lingo that fueled the INTO brand, I thought of a twist of my own: "¡Hola Papi!"

I initially pitched "¡Hola Papi!" as "Queer Latino 'Dear Abby' huffing poppers." It would be more of an advice column spoof than anything else, and it would tackle all the common LGBT issues: dating, insecurities, and petty drama. It was given the green light with some hesitation over the name (it was, after all, inspired by the rampant racial issues on the app, something Grindr probably didn't want to advertise), and up it went.

I just had to hope the letters would come in.

I wasn't sure they actually would, Reader. Grindr itself was, for me, a desperate bid to make connections. I was used to trying to reach out and being met with a palpable silence—"Hello? Hello?" I dreaded that lack of response, and I figured, based on personal history, that my column might be met with a similar quiet.

Also, it was hard to put myself in the shoes of a person who would email their most intimate struggles to a complete stranger over the internet, which is what I was asking people to do. The column was being pushed out through the Grindr app every week, which connected it to the wider gay-sex-having international community, a community I imagined was more interested in trading nudes than in confronting their personal trauma for the sake of generating web content.

Turns out, I was wrong.

In retrospect, it's not that shocking—most people on Grindr were already looking for connection of some kind, someone to talk to and share something intimate with. Wasn't that what had kept me on the app for so many years, the rush of affirmation from a complete stranger, to be desired, to be seen and accepted? I could easily see advice-giving as another form of gay affirmation that, apparently, people needed. The multimillion-dollar sex app had faith in me, sure, but they were more interested in my generating clicks; I wanted to deliver something more, something substantial.

The first letter I answered, fielded from a Twitter follower, hit at the core of what I wanted the column to be: "Hola Papi," it read, "I'm a white guy who has dated almost exclusively brown Latino men. Was I fetishizing them?" My reply was a mix of wry humor with a nugget of wisdom: "No one needs your affirmative action, mija. You were with them because you liked them, and they were with you because they liked you back." I also called him "chipotle mayo," for fun.

Up it went, and then I waited to see what would happen. I assumed some people would like it, and some people would be annoyed that they were receiving an advice column on their hookup app. But at least, I hoped, I would get a few letters.

I didn't receive a few letters, Reader. I got a flood. I knew then that I had tapped into something new and underserved. Of course it was underserved. Hadn't I only recently been in those same shoes, glomming on to more experienced gay men in my desperate bid for a mentor figure?

With that initial deluge of responses, I dared to dream bigger. I dreamed of making a space for the wayward Grindr users of the globe to feel affirmed, understood, and a little less lonely. Not just them, but LGBTQ people around the world. There were letters from everywhere on "the grid": Morocco, India, Brazil, and Japan. The possibilities seemed endless. Ever since I'd first come out, I'd been looking to be a part of something bigger than myself, wanting to connect to my community on a deeper level. Maybe this was it.

And on a professional level, maybe I wouldn't have to worry anymore about having to move back to my parents' house in Oklahoma and return to my job making tortillas after all.

It didn't escape me, however, that I'd initially pitched the column as a spoof. To be clear, I didn't think anybody had any business giving someone else advice, really, unless that person was a doctor or Dolly Parton. To me, advice columns had always felt like a phony enterprise. Who would give a stranger such authority? And, conversely, I couldn't imagine wielding it myself.

"¡Hola Papi!" offered me the chance to poke fun at the larger advice-giving concept as a whole while also giving me an opportunity to "hone my brand," as the youths say.

I was fully prepared to put my jester hat on and jingle-jangle my way through running a column. But almost immediately, the letters got serious. There were letters about being afraid to come out for fear that your family would disown you, letters about being excommunicated from friend and faith groups for being gay or bi or trans.

One in particular has really stuck with me through the years. It arrived during winter, a few months after the column's inauguration. I had ducked into a coffee shop in Chelsea, kicked the snow off my boots, and sat down to pore over my letters, as I often did.

"¡Hola Papi!" it said, as so many of the letters began. "Homosexuality is illegal in my country, but I find myself attracted to a man I work with. I think he might like me back. He is showing me all these signs. Should I tell him how I feel?"

It was in that moment, Reader, that fraudulence hit me like a wave of cinder blocks. I was ill equipped. I quickly realized I had to reassess my goals with this little project; maybe I didn't just want to be a rodeo clown after all.

It's not like I was setting out to be the Latino Harvey Milk with my online column or anything. But I did, at the very least, want to make a worthwhile contribution to the legacy I had inherited, the community I found myself in. And after all my clawing and climbing from rural Oklahoma, I was finally in a perfect position to do so. Now came the part where I had to have something to say, the part where I had to share something with the world, and it seemed like all my vaults were empty. I hadn't done near enough living to be giving anyone advice.

But what was I supposed to do when someone brought me a genuine dilemma like this? Ignore it?

I thought of Erik for the first time in years, from a time in my life when I didn't know up from down or tops from bottoms. I thought of myself sitting on the bench next to him, how small I was then, not in size, but in understanding. Anyone could have told me anything, and I would have believed them. I had taken everything Erik said, for example, as law, simply because he had gotten there first. But really, in retrospect, he was just some random Swedish dude who was probably frustrated that his multiple invitations to hang out in Speedos hadn't registered to me as sexual advances. And yet, through this column I could become someone's Erik: an accidental authority figure. I could hurt somebody if I wasn't careful.

I took stock of myself. Who was I, Reader? Who was I, other than a promiscuous Twitter-addled gay Mexican with chronic anxiety and comorbid mental illnesses who could barely answer his own emails in a timely manner without having a breakdown? Fending for myself kept me busy enough. Did I really have the adequate life experience to be any kind of mentor, to answer letters about complex situations that, in some cases, were literally a matter of life and death?

I tallied up my inadequacies, of which there were many. I thought of the times in my life when I needed help, needed advice, needed a mentor figure to reach down and tell me what I should do. I wondered what such a voice would sound like and what it would say.

Oh goodness, I thought. And then I began my reply.

¡Hola Papi!

How do I let go of my childhood trauma?

Signed,
Damaged Goods

How to Lose a Rabbit

I told myself I was just going to visit the rabbit.

I used to be intimately familiar with the pebbled, bumpy walls of Cache Middle School, where I spent three long, cruel years. I would crouch by them, stare at them, and run my hands over them every morning while waiting for the bell to ring.

Gray, cream, and clay red; I'd pass my time by finding constellations in the wall, connecting pebbles of the same color with my mind's eye to make shapes. I found a teapot, a man wearing a tall hat, a red mass with jagged borders like a continent with coastlines and peninsulas. But my favorite was the rabbit.

This was a rabbit in the loosest sense. Damaged. If I turned my head sideways I could make out the V of its ears, a melting face with one eye resting lower than the other, a black button nose in the center holding the whole project together. I liked to seek him out and spend time with him every morning. I knew exactly where to find him and how to look at him.

As you might have guessed, a child who spent this much time

staring at walls probably wasn't the most popular kid in class. I didn't even make it into the covetable "just kind of there" tier of the middle school hierarchy, which did exist and which I thought of as aspirational. I fell into the exact bottom rung, the standard by which all other rejects were measured.

Many years later, as an adult, I was living in a shoebox (a box for shoes) apartment in New York. One afternoon, my subway car got stuck in the tunnel between Manhattan and Brooklyn, trapping me next to a wild-eyed preacher in a trench coat who took the opportunity to tell me about how the bisexuals were infiltrating the Department of Defense. I decided in that moment that spending some time in the Oklahoma countryside might do me some good. So I booked a flight. I arrived home on a sweltering day in July and found myself compelled to take an overdue pilgrimage to Cache to visit my old friend the rabbit.

Cache has one major road running through it. It was a big deal when we got a stoplight, and an even bigger deal when we got a Sonic Drive-In. Many of the businesses, the ice-cream parlors and arcades, are boarded up. There are almost as many churches as there are residents, some of them operating out of the shells of former establishments. The Burger Shack, for example, an old haunt that was felled by the aforementioned Sonic, now houses a Baptist delegation whose marquee threatens the general public with its weekly take on hell: "Prepare yourself for the lake of fire," it read once. "Cold?" it asked another time on a snowy day in December, when I was visiting for Christmas. "Hell is even colder. Bundle up!" There was a glaring lack of consistency in the institution's perceived temperature of hell.

I wandered through this unchanged town en route to visit the rabbit, stare it in its dumb, droopy face, and finally declare victory over it.

Let me explain, Damaged. At this point in my adult life, things were going pretty well. I had just bought a bed frame for my apartment in Brooklyn, meaning I wouldn't be sleeping on the floor anymore. I had built an online following—not nearly enough to qualify me as "famous" by any stretch, but the number of followers outnumbered the residents of Cache, anyway. I had a full-time job as a writer at Condé Nast, where I had a desk with my name on it on the thirty-first floor of One World Trade Center. My advice column was flourishing. Sometimes I would refresh my in-box just to see the new messages coming in. I had even been in the same room as Anna Wintour once. I dared not meet her gaze, but she was definitely there, and so was I. That's something, I think.

In short, I finally felt big enough, strong enough, to reckon with the place that had caused me so much pain.

The real problems started in the eighth grade. Sixth and seventh grade weren't exactly cakewalks, but they didn't rise to the occasion of "trauma" like eighth grade did, when a skinny white kid with chapped lips named Patty moved into town from out of state. Cache is a place where it's hard to be new. The only people who went to school there were either white farmer kids or Comanche kids, most of whom had known each other since kindergarten. But Patty was different. Patty was an exception.

"Students," our English teacher, a moon-spectacled, silver-haired parody of a schoolmarm named Mrs. Price, announced. "I want you all to meet Patrick." Patrick blinked at us with vacant bug eyes, already bored with the big idea of having to be there. But I immediately saw an opportunity to make a friend. To put it gently, he looked weird enough to be socially attainable. He wore a bright pink hoodie and a baby-blue Tar Heels cap on his head, black shoelaces poking out from holes on top of it like bunny ears. He talked like I had never heard anyone talk, punctuating all his sentences with "fool" and "cuz." Everyone was "fool" and "cuz" to him. *At last*, I thought. *Someone worse than me.*

I didn't bring much to the table in terms of friend potential. Where to begin? People made fun of me for being duck-footed and for, as they put it, "looking like a girl," for having a huge ass and chest. "Boobs," as one budding young scholar described them. I'd once admitted to actively listening to Kelly Clarkson, a miscalculation with devastating results. I had glasses and acne and generally found it difficult to connect with people because of my incredibly off-putting personality, which placed a heavy emphasis on what I saw as my sole redeeming quality: I was smart.

I needed everyone to know I was smart, because what else did I have? I sucked at sports. I wasn't funny. I didn't even have a charming self-awareness of my plight that could play out as self-deprecation; I didn't make fat jokes at my own expense or pretend to flirt with girls I had no chance with for other people's entertainment. It's not that I didn't know what I was. I did. But I was desperate not to be that, and it showed. Showing off that I could solve a math problem at the board while Brent McWhoever couldn't was equal parts small revenge and a desperate attempt to submit just one positive feature of the mess that was me. Let me tell you, Damaged, it did not work. All it achieved was making me, well, unpleasant.

I had been a colossal disappointment from the moment I'd set foot in Cache. My parents, who'd gone to school there, had been basketball stars. I had inherited none of these skills, as my many losses to my dad at HORSE attested (he never let me win and indeed seemed to take great pleasure in trouncing me).

Teachers who'd either had them in class or been their classmates would squint at me and ask, "You Brammer's kid?" as if there must have been some sort of mistake. Tired of eating lunch alone and whiling away my free time crouching behind the school building and looking for rodent faces in a pebbled wall, I developed a singular goal of becoming Patty's friend.

Patty and I had two classes together. One was English with Mrs. Price, the other was drama with Ms. Nelson, a rail-thin middle-aged woman with thick, crumbly eye makeup and a chain-smoker's voice who identified herself as divorced on our first day of school. Our assignments were pulled out of an ancient workbook with missing pages that saw us improvising roles like "homeless werewolf" and "cowboy who's afraid of cows."

It quickly became clear that Patty was born for the stage. When given a role, his gangly, unwieldy body would snap into discipline, becoming an instrument through which he would channel the very essence of his roles, like "clown with Tourette's syndrome" or "courtroom lawyer who's secretly a golden retriever." *Ladies and gentlemen of the jury, please rub my belly.*

This was a problem for me, as Patty's skill propelled him into popularity and far out of reach for my friendship. In fact, it didn't take long for Patty to become one of the most popular kids in school. Far from being mocked as "gay" for wearing pink, as any other boy would and should have been, people began to emulate his style. Even the farmer kids began to wear his baby blues, his soft pinks, and his chunky Adidas sneakers. They started listening to Eminem. They even started calling each other "fool," all because Patty had charmed them, had made them laugh.

Overnight, Patty developed a clique. There was Ashton, a short, angry kid who glared at the world through a perpetual squint, probably because he was in middle school and a boy and his parents had named him Ashton. There was Dillon, a tall, lumbering future farmer of America with bright red hair whom everyone called "Hammy." It wasn't a fat joke, more a cruel observation of his face, which was piglike with its flat nose and pink cheeks. There was Trish, the short, rude daughter of the Spanish teacher, Ms. Gonzalez, whom every red-blooded heterosexual male in the building, student or otherwise, had a crush on. Then there was Trey, the giggly bucktoothed son of a former mayor whose last name was plastered around town, in the park and on the football stadium and such, because his family had money.

All in all, it wasn't exactly a dream team. And yet Patty's touch, his very decision to surround himself with these people, had transformed them. He'd made them exotic and interesting. Surely if someone as clever as Patty had seen something in these individuals, then their positive qualities had simply been overlooked.

The first time I ventured to approach them was during lunch. "Hello," I said, setting my tray down on the long table. "What's up?"

"Sup," Patty said, though it felt like he hadn't seen me.

"We're in drama together," I said while Ashton and Trish stared daggers into me. "You were funny as the garbage collector yesterday."

"Thanks, cuz," he said, before repeating his standout line. "I'm not a garbage boy, I'm a garbage *man*." The table all but applauded.

I sat frozen, terrified that whatever came out of my mouth next would betray me and ruin everything. Friendship was so foreign to me that I saw it as a matter of scoring points, of saying the right thing at the right time and meeting an imaginary quota of jokes. "Garbage, ha, ha," was what I said.

Day after day, I continued to sit down next to Patty and his crew, hoping something might happen through sheer exposure. It sort of did. He learned my name and would give me a nod in the hallways. We started doing skits together in drama class, and to my surprise I found I actually enjoyed being up in front of everyone and making a fool of myself.

One of our skits together was a short romantic comedy. We were both bachelors pining over the same woman, played by Laura Beth, a shy girl who wore her thick brown hair in ropy braids and who would occasionally disappear from school to help her parents with "the harvest" until one harvest when she failed to return at all. "Oh gawsh," she said to absolutely everything.

Patty and I were to one-up each other in a bid for Laura Beth's affections, she being the daughter of a wealthy businessman in this skit, though she retained the name "Laura Beth" in it for some reason, perhaps because it was such an apt, all-encompassing name for her. Patty wanted her for love, whereas my motivation was her money.

It was a brief window into what I imagined was Patty's world. Up in front of everyone, I felt I had escaped my hated body, escaped my status as a wannabe, and for a moment I was free as a fool, tasked with nothing but making people laugh. "Laura Beth," I pleaded. "I love you with all my heart. From your hair to your brrrrrrooowww*green* eyes! Yes, your beautiful green eyes."

"Oh gawsh," Laura Beth said.

"He may very well love you, Laura Beth," Patty chimed in. "But can he do *this*?" He slowly dropped into the splits with a pained, tortured expression on his face. Everyone in the room nearly doubled over.

It was the first time Patty's magic had rubbed off on me, and I understood it then, the transformative powers of this strange new person. He'd done the impossible. He'd brought me out of my shell.

Time went on, and our passion for the stage brought Patty and me closer together. We even started chatting over AOL Instant Messenger. His profile had this list of names of people he liked from school, written in Comic Sans in different neon colors that corresponded to their personalities. I wasn't on it, but I saw it as my mission to get there. If I could prove to him that I was funny, that I was worth his time, then maybe I'd have a friend, as commemorated by my name in neon on his AIM profile page. Maybe mine would be blue.

The first time we hung out together after school, we played video games. I was all jitters before he arrived, cleaning things up, but not making anything too clean, lest I be seen as a neat freak, which I supposed wouldn't be cool. The doorbell rang. "Sup, cuz," he said.

We played *Halo*. We tried to do multiplayer online at first, but my house out in the middle of the countryside had a terrible internet connection. We would freeze up, glitch out, and every time it happened the other players would call us fags via their headsets and tell us to log off, and Patty would violently curse. I felt guilty, as if this were entirely my fault for living where I did, and then I got angry at my house, which was frankly ruining everything.

We decided to play one-on-one offline instead. I don't know why I assumed Patty would destroy me at *Halo*. I guess I figured Patty was better than me at everything. But in the first round, I got ahold of a sword, sneaked up on him from behind, and won the match by stabbing him.

"*FUCK!*" Patty yelled. He threw the controller on the ground, sending the batteries flying out. I was frozen, afraid that anything I said might further incriminate me.

"Sorry," he said. He took a sharp breath through his teeth, picked up the controller, and put the batteries back in. "Let's go again." I made sure to let him win that time.

I came away from that evening thinking I had screwed it all up. I chastised myself for being unable to just be normal. I'd seen other guys interact with each other. I knew that when Patty threw the controller, the "guy" thing to do would have been to call him a pussy, shove him, and curse right back at him. But that wasn't me. I was too soft. I was always too soft.

The thing was, I wasn't just looking for a friend in Patty—I was looking for someone to teach me how to be a boy. My effeminate mannerisms had earned me scorn throughout my middle school years. I was always wearing the wrong things, liking the wrong things, walking wrong, talking wrong, wrong, wrong, wrong, and every time I was wrong, I had to hear about it.

Patty, on the other hand, moved through life differently. When he did things, they became okay, even if they hadn't been okay before. His slang, his clothes, his attitude—I wanted to emulate these things because I wanted to move that way, too: easier, lighter, better. The difference wasn't that he was following the rules better. The difference was that he made his own rules. That's what being a boy was about: dominance. Dominance over the rules, over the space around you, over the person next to you. I might not, in a million years, have been like that myself. But I could at the very least try to be more like Patty.

Wanting to be more like Patty was why I asked my mom for a Tar Heels shirt I had seen in the mall for my fourteenth birthday. It was black with baby-blue letters. I'd never seen a Tar Heels game in my life. I barely even knew what sport they played, and to be honest the name kind of put me off. I didn't want tar on *my* heel and I didn't know why anyone would. But I asked for it because of how desperately I wanted to be one of the boys.

Certainly, what happened next wasn't entirely because of the shirt, Damaged. But it incited the event that launched my troubles. I wore it to school once or twice. Then, just after winter, when the mornings were chilly and the afternoons were hot, I walked up to join Patty, Ashton, and Trish where they had grouped up by the wall outside. Right when I got there, Ashton had a devious look on his face. It was clear they had been discussing me.

"Hey, Patty," Ashton said with a knowing nudge and a wink. "Shirts."

"Shirts," Patty agreed with a smirk.

As it turned out, my Tar Heels fashion moment hadn't gone overlooked by Patty and company. "Did you get that shirt because you like him?" Ashton asked smugly, rounding on me. "Do you have a crush?"

A crush?

The thought had never crossed my mind, and if it had tried to I would have run it over immediately, backed up, then run it over again. To me, there was no such thing as a boy having a crush on a boy, it being such an unthinkable taboo. When I thought about Patty, I thought about approval: a person with the authority to look at me and say, "You're good." But there was no explaining that to Ashton.

"What?" was all I could muster in self-defense.

"Are you in love with him?" Ashton pressed on while Patty suppressed a devious giggle fit, sanctioning the inquisition. "Are you some kind of faggot? Huh?"

"No," I said. Answering the question in earnest was itself incriminating. Only a faggot, you see, would ever have to deny being a faggot.

The bell rang, and not knowing what else to do, I trailed behind them into the building, though their backs were turned to me, clearly a symbolic recognition of their decision to antagonize me from here on out. My head was ringing as if I'd been sucker punched. Wrong, wrong, wrong, I was being wrong again. But if I couldn't be myself, and I couldn't be a discount version of the other boys, then what was I supposed to do? Who was I even allowed to be at all?

I tried to sit down at our typical lunch spot that day, even after that terrible morning, because it was what I had done every day. The cafeteria was serving hot dogs. No sooner had I taken my seat than Dillon took his hot dog out of the bun. He slapped it across my face and rubbed it along my cheek. "Do you like wieners?" he said while I sat there. "Faggots like wieners, right?"

This day would not end up being an anomaly.

I was called a faggot every day from then on out. When I walked down the hall, Dillon or Patty would put their arm around me, hug me in close, and whisper it in my ear. They'd ask me if I liked being touched like that, and then they'd shove me and tell me to get away from them, disgusted by the words they'd put in my mouth, by the touch I hadn't asked for. I started to fear walking to my locker, then walking to school, then coming to school at all. Some teachers witnessed it. Ms. Gonzalez saw Ashton slap my books out of my hands once and offered a weak "Hey!" in response. Principal Watts, a no-nonsense woman with glasses and the general demeanor of a hawk, knew what was happening. "Well," she said. "Boys are like that."

My parents could tell that I'd stopped eating, sleeping, and doing my homework. I was failing classes I'd always gotten A's in. I didn't tell them anything because I thought it would out me as gay. I wondered if being bullied in the first place was some sort of failure of my own masculinity, evidence that I was weak, that I deserved it. Sometimes my dad would drive me to school in the mornings, and I would beg him to let me be late, to let me stay in his car a while longer. I would feel sick in the mornings out of anxiety.

I started spending my lunch period in the auditorium on the stage behind a heavy velvet curtain. I remember how the floor felt, the way the dirt on it pressed into my palms and left little red indents, the way my feet made loud, echoing thumps as I situated myself on the ground. One time the janitor opened the door to clean up, and I was so scared he'd find me that I nearly dry heaved.

Patty, Dillon, Trey, and Ashton, meanwhile, took to waiting around for me outside the school building. They prank-called my house. They told everyone I was gay. Most days, I was called "faggot" more than my actual name. I started having suicidal thoughts—nothing tangible, but I flirted with the warm notion of relief, with the idea of not being. Entertaining that fantasy kept me going. It made me feel in control of my life, even if only for fleeting moments.

Our big project for drama class was the spring play, a series of comedy skits loosely held together under the umbrella of "funny." There was a Barbie-and-Ken skit, in which the gag was that Ken and Barbie wanted a divorce but had to keep up appearances for their plastic friends. There was a movie spoof based on *The Little Mermaid*, in which she was half crab instead of half fish. "Don't mess with me, I'm feeling crabby!" she said at one pivotal point. There was a skit about Italian mobsters in a pizza shop, the only one I appeared in, with my breakout role of "Mobster #3." My one line was "A wise guy, eh?" Compelling stuff.

Patty was cast as the star in all five skits, to no one's surprise. In the days leading up to the big production, we were expected to stay after school to rehearse. I told Ms. Nelson that I had only one line, and that I pretty much had it down, and asked if I could please be excused. I didn't want to spend any more time around Patty than I had to. "It will count against your final grade," Ms. Nelson said, a condition I eagerly accepted.

On the night of the play, I donned my dad's pinstripe blazer, three sizes too big for me, and a bowler hat my mom had picked up for me at the thrift shop. Onstage, I pointed at Patty with a fake gun over the red-and-white tablecloth in the imaginary Italian restaurant. "A wise guy, eh?" I sneered. I didn't anticipate any Tony nominations.

A problem arose with the *Little Mermaid* spoof. The giant papier-mâché clam—a key prop—wouldn't open. Its lips had accidentally been glued shut. Ms. Nelson urged Patty to go out and entertain the audience in front of the curtain while she and a student pried it open. I was backstage, watching Ms. Nelson and Mobster #2 jointly try to jimmy open the prop with Ms. Nelson's car keys while Patty worked the crowd. I don't know what he said, but I heard laughter and thunderous applause. I had some idea of what he was doing: making those confident gestures that conducted people's response however he liked.

Standing there behind the curtains, I wondered if it would make any difference if the audience knew about me, about what was happening to me, if knowing would make them care, if it would make them stop cheering. But how would they ever know? I stood in rigid silence, watching that stupid clam slowly lose its fight.

The following Monday, back in homeroom, Mrs. Price pulled a small cardboard box out from under her desk. "I want to congratulate everyone who participated in the play on Friday. I decided to get your autographs now, before you get famous," she said.

She shuffled around with her box full of thin strips of paper, dutifully placing one on the desk of every thespian in the room who'd been in the class production. She arrived at me and set my little slip on my desk. I couldn't help but feel I was being mocked. *A wise guy, eh?* How did she remember I had been in the play at all? I would have preferred she skipped me.

Then she arrived at Patty's desk. He was staring out into space, as was his custom in class—chin resting on his knuckles, baseball cap sitting askew on his head. Mrs. Price stopped in front of him, took a good, long look, as if on the verge of saying something stern and punishing. She raised the cardboard box over her head and then dumped its contents down over him, sending a flurry of white slips of paper fluttering to earth. Some of the students in class started clapping. *Well,* I thought. *Time to kill myself.*

It wasn't so much that I wanted the praise Patty was getting, though of course it would have been nice. It was more that in that moment, everything became clear as a crystal bullet to me. Patty could call me a faggot every day, he could make my life a living hell, and everyone could see it and know about it and people would still love him because I didn't matter. Those slips of paper were a prophecy. He was going to be famous. He was going to be a rich and successful comedian, or an actor, or something, and Mrs. Price would frame one of his autographs and put it up in her room and tell people about it years later. And what about me? What would happen to me?

My parents kept a pistol under their bed. After school, I told them I wasn't feeling well and I didn't want to join them at Pizza Hut, an unprecedented move on my part. When they left, I crawled under their bed and retrieved the gun. It was much heavier than I expected, like the iron core of a tiny planet with a lethal gravity.

I walked up to the mirror and held the gun to my head, just to see what it looked like, if it was as silly looking and melodramatic as it felt. It was. I was like the fake mobster: drowning in an adult costume several sizes too big for me, holding a ridiculous prop. I didn't know how to load it or if there were even bullets in it. I didn't know anything. Wrong, wrong, always wrong. I cried over all the things I couldn't do and slid the gun back into its place.

In May, there was a day called "field day"—the worst day of my young life—traditionally when the eighth-graders, who would be high schoolers soon, would get half the day off to hang out on the soccer field, eat pizza, and sign yearbooks. I was walking toward the bleachers when a soccer ball flew toward me and hit my thigh, narrowly missing my groin, leaving a sting where it had landed. "He doesn't even have a dick," Ashton, the kicker, announced. "He's a girl."

I knew better than to engage. I turned around and headed back toward the school. The soccer field was up on a hill, and as I was descending I felt a hand on my back. I tripped, and I hit the dirt. I got up and dusted myself off to see Ashton, Dillon, Trey, and Patty. Trey was giggling. Something about his giggling made me angrier with him than with the others—he was just going along with it, simply grateful to be a part of something. I saw myself the most in that. Would I have been him if given the chance? I felt mocked by the very thought, both because it didn't matter—I'd never know—

and because it robbed me of the one thing that could give me some solace, the idea that I was purely and entirely a victim.

Blind with rage, I walked toward him ready to fight, not caring if I got beat up, when to my surprise he began walking backward. Ashton, though barking insults, was also backing away. I didn't understand. After everything that had happened, they didn't want to fight me. Wasn't that what people who hated each other wanted to do?

"You better back the hell up," Ashton said in his retreat. A small crowd had gathered around us and was following us to the school building in our awkward chase, me, walking just fast enough to be threatening, him, retreating just slow enough to not look like an entire coward. I could feel myself becoming a spectacle, could feel my peers anticipating something delicious and wild, a fight or a breakdown, but I didn't care so much anymore.

I was dizzy from mania when we got to the middle school. All hope of walking out of this day like it was any other day was gone, which made it all the easier for me to escalate. I heard Patty shouting, somewhere behind me, screaming, "Let me go!" Two kids were holding him back. "I'm going to kill this faggot!"

He hadn't been talking like that before he was being held back, of course. All along, all that talk, and none of it had been real. I could have fought back at any point. That made it worse. It made it so much worse.

I remember what followed in fuzzy snapshots—being pulled into the building by two of my classmates and being set down in the hall, banging my head into the lockers, so hard that my vision blacked out with every clanging, thundering smack, crying and saying over and over again that I wanted to die. I remember saying so made one of my classmates cry. I remember, still remember, think of often, one kid, a baseball player named David, bending down and saying, "I'm gonna kick their asses, bro."

Principal Watts arrived, cold and all business, and set me down in her office. Then, to my horror, she brought in Trey, Ashton, Dillon, and Patty, leading them into the room with me and setting them down on chairs directly across from me.

"You all stay put," she said gruffly. "I'll be right back." She left the room and closed the door behind her. Panicking, I launched myself at the door, thinking something terrible might happen to me if I stayed in there alone. I banged on it like a trapped animal until she returned. "What on earth is wrong with you?" she asked. She grabbed me by the arm and set me down in a separate room.

I waited there for what felt like forever. When she came back, I saw that the boys were no longer sitting in her office. She sat down and folded her arms in front of her on the desk. "I heard," she said solemnly, "that you were talking about killing yourself."

It didn't register to me that this shouldn't have been the focus of her inquiry. I had only admitted to wanting to kill myself minutes ago, and they had been torturing me for weeks. But I accepted it.

"Yes," I said.

"Do you want to kill yourself?" she asked.

"Yes," I said.

She sighed and picked up the phone. She called my mother, who answered. "Your son has had a rough day," Principal Watts said.

When I got home, my mother was in tears. "Suicide?" she said.

My abuelos, drawn from the couch by the commotion, walked over to listen. "Suicide?" my abuela asked my abuelo in her accent, as if it were a word she'd never encountered before. He muttered something to her, I assume explaining what "suicide" meant, or what it meant for us.

I was hollowed out. My body was crying and shaking, but I was somewhere else. My mother was pacing, hand over her mouth. She knew everyone in that town, and everyone knew her. "Do you know how fast this kind of shit gets around?" she asked me.

"Yes," I said.

"Why?" she asked, addressing the core of the thing.

"I don't know," I lied.

"Are you gay?" she asked, and it wasn't a question out of nowhere. Indeed, it felt like the most appropriate question in the world at the time, because I knew what she meant. It was how I understood "gay" then, too: are you doing this, are you acting this way, are you so difficult and troubled, because you're not quite right?

"No," I lied through my sobs. I pretended it was entirely out of the question. "I'm not." A quiet descended like a thick blanket of snow. The enormity of the situation overwhelmed us, my mother, my abuelos, and I, and so we wordlessly decided to go through the motions of a regular afternoon.

"We're going to eat," my mother said plainly.

I got in the car, and we went to a buffet. When I got out, the wind caught the door and it hit the car parked next to ours. A woman with long curly hair and sunglasses on rolled down her window. "Hey!" she shouted at me. "Watch what you're doing!"

My mother pounced on her like a hawk on a snake. "HEY!"

she said, louder and in mockery of how the woman had said it. "It was an *accident*. You don't know what kind of day he's had!" She was using her familiar *I'm a proud Mexican woman and I am going to kill you* voice, a voice I was familiar with. But she was shaking, I noticed, something my mother did not do. She was not a person who cried or a person who exposed any weaknesses. But here she was, overcome, more upset than I'd ever seen her. "You leave him alone, you understand me?"

I lay down on my bed that night with my eyes open, unable to sleep, unsure how I was ever supposed to sleep again.

I would have to return to school the following Monday, knowing that by then everyone would think of me as the kid who'd announced that he wanted to kill himself. My dad dropped me off at the last possible minute before the bell rang so I wouldn't have to loiter outside. I marched into my first-period class, holding my books tight to my chest. It felt like slow motion, walking past all those people who knew I'd wanted to kill myself. They looked at me and then quickly looked away, pity and shame, and I was left with the impossible task of continuing: not as if nothing had happened, but as if things could change.

That was how the rest of my school year went. I was a ghost. People were polite to me in a sterile, obligatory way, as if I might jump off a building and blame them for it if they said the wrong thing. Patty, Dillon, Ashton, Trey, and Trish didn't so much as look in my direction. That was all just fine by me.

One weekend before summer break, my mother asked me if I wanted ice cream. "Sure," I said, and she took me to Braum's, got us two ice-cream cones, and stopped the car in the parking lot.

"Buddy," she said, weighing her words. "I'm sorry." In terms of how wild a thing this was to hear from my mother, it was roughly on par with her saying "I've decided to join the circus." It wasn't that my mother was uncaring or anything. Indeed, she was one of the most caring people I'd ever met. It was more that, back then, especially, she was a severe person who would never articulate a sentiment like that in quite that way, much like a piranha would probably not give you a smooch.

"I didn't protect you," she said. "I wasn't on your side when that happened, and that wasn't right. I was wrong. I'm so, so sorry."

"It's okay," I said, licking my ice cream, unsure what to do with this kind of energy out of my mother.

"No," she said. "It's not."

I paused, put my ice cream down, and said, "Thank you."

"I want you to make a decision," she went on. "Do you want to come to Lawton High with me?" That was the school in town, "the city," as some called it, where she taught English. I told her that yes, I did.

Many of the specifics have left me since then, Damaged. At times a familiar smell will shock me back into that period of my life, those hallways, that place, and I'll feel like throwing up. For years I had nightmares about being back there, and even when my life felt good and my past was behind me, I still felt the profound effect of eighth grade. That time of my life shaped the economy of my emotions. For a long time, even playful jokes about me felt like attacks that endangered my life. I'd strike back, overcompensate, and intentionally injure anyone who'd unintentionally injured me. I mistrusted authority figures who claimed to want to help me. I thought every single friend I ever had was waiting to abandon me, to turn into a tormentor.

Trauma lives in the body long after the events that birthed it go away. It builds a home for itself in our memories, where it asserts itself as reality: I was treated this way because there is something wrong with me, and if I am to protect myself, then I must carry a healthy, vigilant sense of paranoia with me at all times. Never again, it says.

The architecture of my entire life was built around that "never again." Everything down to the things I ate, the friends I made, the way I talked, and the way I walked, they all, to some degree, took "never again" into account. When I decided to lose weight by running several miles every day, sometimes to the point of nearly fainting, I would remind myself: *Never again*. When I got tired of working, when I found myself starting to slip with my grades, I would think *Never again*, and I would drive myself harder.

As I arrived at Cache Middle School on that hot day in July, awards and success and power in hand, I couldn't help but feel a little foolish at how much smaller everything was than I'd remembered. The sidewalks, the tables out front, the campus itself; I had made this place the very center of my life, and all along, all this time, it had been small. So small that I couldn't imagine these things as the looming monuments to dread they had once been. I sat myself down at one of the tables and tried with all my might to be a kid again, hooking my fingers into the plastic mesh of the tabletop like I used to, wanting to conjure that familiar hurt so that I might address it. But it was no good.

I approached the pebbled wall where the rabbit lived, where I used to sit and wait for the bell. I looked for him. I crouched down, reasoning that I had grown taller since I'd last seen it. I searched and searched and searched. But I couldn't find the rabbit.

We can't change the events of our lives. They happened, and there they are. But the lines we draw to connect those events, the shapes we make and the conclusions we reach, those come from us. They are our own design.

Is there a way of looking at the narrative arc of your life differently, Damaged? Are you aware it's a narrative at all, one with a beginning, middle, and end that you wrote yourself?

That doesn't mean the bad things that happened weren't real or important. But we're human beings. We understand the world through stories. My middle school was my antagonist, the big bad wolf that I would have to spend my whole life getting strong enough to overcome. But it was just a building. It hadn't been watching over me, taunting me, pushing me to work harder. It had just been sitting there.

Trauma is always trying to convince us that we are beings trapped in amber, defined by the static, unchangeable events of our lives. But that's not the case. The worst things that have ever happened to us don't define us. We are the ones who get to define what those things mean. I hope the next time you revisit the mosaic of your life, Damaged, you take the time to tilt your head. You might find something new.

¡Hola Papi!

How do I make peace with the years
I lost in the closet?

Signed,
Wasted Time

How to Kiss Your Girlfriend

I met Rebecca on MySpace. She had a widget on her page that allowed anonymous commenters to share their thoughts, because tweens are nothing if not self-destructive. "You're an ugly slut," one commenter wrote. I gallantly responded, "I don't think you're ugly. You're very pretty!"

I wasn't going to be knighted anytime soon, Wasted, but I really did think she was pretty. Rebecca had long brown hair and an apple-cheeked smile, and I liked the way she dressed. Scrolling through her pictures, I noticed she would cycle through punk band shirts and preppy sweaters without fully committing to either aesthetic. I thought this was a bold sartorial vision.

One night, while I was fully immersed in my typical routine of playing around on Photoshop on the family desktop computer, I checked my typically lifeless MySpace. I was surprised to see I had a private message from Rebecca. "Hey!" she had written back. "I just wanted to say thank you. That was really sweet of you to say."

I must admit that message got my heart racing. Cliché as it is, it must be said that Rebecca was a cheerleader, and I was like most middle to high schoolers who operated in rote hierarchies beaten to death by movies. That Rebecca would pay me, an ambiguously Latin potato, any attention at all was pretty staggering. "Of course," I replied. "And hey, I meant it!"

I was an incoming high school freshman. At that point, I'd never been in a romantic relationship that I hadn't completely fabricated as part of my imaginary reality TV arc. I hadn't even entertained the notion. Not only was I, in a word, ugly, but I also couldn't quite get myself to think of girls in the way I was supposed to.

I thought of girls as allies, inasmuch as they weren't as terrible as boys, and I thought of them as possessing some method of living that I was jealous of: going to the bathroom together, caring about what they smelled like, putting together outfits—all things I would eventually discover weren't inherently feminine, really, but activities that sounded like great fun I was missing out on. I preferred not to dwell on whether this had to do with feelings I had about boys, as doing so made me sad.

So it surprised me when Rebecca continued to message me that summer before I went to Lawton High. My mom was transferring me there after I'd nearly been bullied to death in Cache. We lived so far from Lawton High that I wouldn't have been able to attend at all if my mom weren't an English teacher there. That also meant there was a good chance no one at Lawton High would know about the reputation I'd built in Cache as "the probably-gay kid who wanted to kill himself." Seeing an opportunity for reinvention, I went about planning who I was going to be. Getting a girlfriend had never been in my equations—that was dreaming too big.

"Hey again," she wrote the very next day. "How's your summer? I'm so bored."

"Hi," I wrote back. "Ugh. Bored here too. My uncle is taking me fishing tomorrow. Gone fishing! Ha ha. Anyway, tell me more about you!"

I found out Rebecca was mad at her parents a lot but still saw herself as a daddy's girl. Her mom was always pressuring her to be more feminine and to get more involved in student government. She liked to wear black and she liked metal bands, but she liked "pretty things" too. "Maybe I'm a girly girl at heart! I don't know," she wrote. "Ha."

We were in the age of the cluttered, blinkering social media profile. These profiles were festooned with GIFs and often featured a curated playlist. Looking at Rebecca's page—neon hearts and metal music, emotional expressions like "she's slow to trust, but when she falls she falls hard"—I was enchanted. She had pictures of herself at cheer meets and with her best friends, tongues out, giving the camera the middle finger. I couldn't believe I was entering this person's orbit. I dared to imagine what it might be like to see myself on this page, a cherished fragment of this chaotic, alluring digital document.

Our online conversations carried on through my first weeks at school. Rebecca was in the grade below me and was in her last year in the middle school in Lawton. We hadn't met in person yet, but we enjoyed this tragic distance between us. It gave us something mutual to hate. "Ugh," she'd message me. "I wish we could have eaten lunch together today. I have so much to tell you."

"I had the worst day," I'd reply. "Where do I even start?"

It was exciting to fill our days with the mundane, the annoying, and the outrageous just to have something to share with each other later. It made being at a bigger, more chaotic school where I knew no one more tolerable.

Lawton High wasn't short on drama. Within my first few weeks, I saw a student physically fight our vice principal, a white-haired tree of a man who looked like Gandalf if Gandalf had spent ten years in an American prison. He found a worthy opponent in Francesca, who was four feet tall and using plastic trays as projectiles. He eventually subdued her by picking her up. She bit his hand and drew blood.

There were hallway fights galore, and every classroom was falling apart. An entire chalkboard crumbled and fell to the ground during our first day of math class, and our teacher openly wept in front of us.

I looked forward to all these things, because they gave me something interesting to tell Rebecca about privately.

Soon these chats got too big for MySpace, and we decided to start talking with each other over the phone. "Hey!" she said the first time I called. There was a roughness to her voice I liked. It made her sound like a bartender or a heavy smoker. "So . . . yeah. Hi."

We would talk every day for hours: about the minutiae of our day, our families, the lives we'd lived so far. We couldn't talk during school, so we started writing notes to each other on paper, vowing to exchange them when we finally met in person. I felt positively giddy over our budding relationship.

Look, Wasted, I had a vague idea that I was gay. Although I'd never, ever used that word. I thought of myself more as "a person with unique difficulty accessing heterosexuality." Even when I was alone at night, with the family computer all to myself, armed with technological knowledge my parents didn't have, I only dared to look at straight porn. I'd end up focusing mostly on the man. The woman was there to grant me safe passage, like Charon ferrying me across the horny river Styx.

For better or worse, I did see in Rebecca an opportunity to be "correct." If I could be with Rebecca—if I could love Rebecca—I could avoid having to be a homosexual, something that, as I'd learned in Cache, was an incorrect thing to be. But first Rebecca would have to actually like me in that way, and although she seemed to be interested, meeting in person could change that pretty quickly. She would at some point have to look at me, after all.

When it came time to meet, we decided to do what most kids our age did: hang out at the mall. This was an entirely viable way to spend an afternoon back then; teens would make the rounds on the weekend, never buying anything, hoping that they'd run into friends and nemeses, opportunities to stir up minor scandals that would sustain them through the school week.

My mom dropped me off at the entrance and told me to have fun. I was sporting my weekend attire, a Green Day band tee and Aéropostale jeans. But my killer outfit failed to give me confidence. Standing there, waiting for Rebecca in front of Claire's, I felt mocked by my own hopes.

She arrived—shorter than I'd expected, wearing a green cheer ribbon in her hair and a Linkin Park shirt. She seemed lost for a moment, her eyes avidly scanning the crowd looking for me, and I felt a pang of embarrassment to be the disappointment I was sure to be. I made my way to her, each step heavy as a falling piano. Her eyes met mine, and her posture relaxed. *There you are*, she seemed to say.

Already, this was huge for me, Wasted. In my not-so-distant middle school life, the best I could hope for was not to be outright detested. To have someone want to see me, really *want* to see me, was new. I waved, and she ran up to me and gave me a hug, her arms wrapping around my waist. "Finally!" she said.

I felt unconditional warmth, a safety so complete I forgot why I had ever been worried. I could have wept. "Finally," I agreed. We walked hand in hand through the mall. We traded the notes we'd written, so many notes, and promised not to open them until we were both at home, something I couldn't wait to do so I could enjoy everything that had transpired in private, where I could assure myself that it had indeed happened and it wouldn't go away.

Life turned to gold, Wasted. It felt like the sun was always shining on me at just the right angle. Rebecca and I would talk on the phone every night, and sometimes we'd fall asleep like that. I had opened her notes, each one lit up with colors and drawings of flowers, annotated with smiley faces and arrows pointing to a part I should read next. Rebecca's liking me that much, liking me enough to write me all these elaborately decorated notes, made it easier for me to like myself. *A girl likes me*, I would privately affirm on a daily basis. *Oh wow, a girl likes me.*

And I liked her back.

But it was a complicated kind of affection. Even if it didn't feel complicated back then. No, if anything, Wasted, it felt like the easiest thing in the world to return Rebecca's warmth. I'd make little drawings in the margins of my notes. I told her how excited I was to see her again. I was happy when she was happy, and I was fiercely supportive whenever she told me that someone had slighted her in some way: scuffles in student leadership, cheer drama. But the relationship itself, the shape it took and the way it functioned, was complicated nonetheless because I was, irrevocably and in the end, a latent homosexual who was just doing his best to make it work, as Tim Gunn of *Project Runway* would say (again, gay).

"Do you, uh, want to be my girlfriend?" I asked her over the phone on the night of Thanksgiving.

"I, uh," she said, mocking the way I'd asked, "definitely do."

A Person with a Girlfriend. This was an identity I treasured, held tight to my chest, and carried with me as one might a particularly hard-won license. Having this license exempted me from many unpleasant things: intrusive questions about my sexuality, self-loathing over being single, and the existential dread of wondering if I would die alone (a favorite activity of mine at fourteen). These dreaded specters would knock on my door, and I would flash them my "Person with a Girlfriend" license, and they would apologize and move along.

Back then I didn't dare imagine life as something I could control. None of my experiences lent themselves to that conclusion. My primary goal, instead, was comfort—to make the pangs of life a little more bearable, to be able to withstand its fits and starts until it ferried me to death. It wasn't just about how I lived but also about how I dreamed, what I would allow myself to fantasize about having. For the most part, this began and ended at "good enough." It made perfect sense for me to stay where I was, to invest even more in Rebecca and me.

Our first real date that wasn't roaming around the mall was at the movies. We were going to see *Harry Potter and the Goblet of Fire*. I knew that being in a dark room together meant we would probably have to kiss. I'd never kissed anyone before, though I did have a blurry notion of how it worked. My concern was that when we kissed, she would somehow pick up on the one thing in our flourishing romance that wasn't quite right: as pretty as I thought she was, the visceral, physical attraction wasn't there.

When I arrived, I found Rebecca waiting for me in an oversized sweater. We took our seats and held hands as the previews rolled. I hoped she didn't notice how nervous I was. "Have you read the book?" she asked.

"What book?" I said. "Oh, Harry Potter. Yes. I've read the book."

"I haven't," she said. "I've been waiting forever just to get the rest of the story since the last movie. Isn't that dumb? Why don't I just read the books?"

"Yeah," I said. I leaned over, and kissing wasn't at all what I had imagined it to be like. It felt sort of like falling into someone else's face with your face, only the faces stopped being faces and became something else, something more important and encompassing. There was a brief moment of frightening gravity before impact. And then it happened, and we kissed, and I thought life would be good from that moment on.

We kissed through the film, and kissed goodbye, and when I went home I lay in bed wishing that this could be the end of my movie. I was good here. Roll credits. But of course, life isn't like that until you literally die, and so my happy fuzzy thoughts turned to the future: Okay, so Rebecca and I would have to get married now, right? And sometime before that, we would have to have sex?

Where I'm from, Wasted, it was entirely common to be married before you could legally drink. My own parents had met as sophomores in high school. Classmates would occasionally get pregnant, causing a minor scandal, but it was all part of the cultural paradox we were so accustomed to: sex outside of marriage was bad and sinful, but if you hadn't had sex by sixteen, well, what's the holdup, fella? You gay or somethin'? (Probably!)

I didn't get any sex education from the nuns in Catholic grade school, who found the entire business of pickle tickling so outrageous that it ought not even to be referenced. In middle school, Coach Patton, a lazy math teacher with a potbelly who also taught an ill-defined class called Physical Health, outsourced his duties to us seventh-graders, telling us each to pick a sex-ed topic and then present on it in front of the class. I was tasked with educating my peers on the colorful subject of "the vagina," which I pronounced "vuh-guy-na" in front of everyone.

All this is to say, Wasted, that both Rebecca and I figured we would need to have sex sooner rather than later now that we were boyfriend and girlfriend, a prospect that utterly terrified me. I had just figured out how to kiss someone. Everything I knew about sex, I knew about from low-production-value porn where I mostly stared at the guy's pecs and pretended nothing was happening below that.

Nevertheless, Rebecca and I introduced sex to our regular conversations. "Dirty talk," I suppose I would call it, in which I attempted to say hot things like "I want to take your pants off." Bleak.

After we crossed that Rubicon, I engaged in a delicate dance. I had a feeling I couldn't give Rebecca everything she would need, but I wanted to try, and so in fits and starts, I tried. During her birthday party in March, Rebecca's mom, a wrinkled smoker with clumpy mascara, asked us to please "stop being so touchy-feely" with each other. Such was my commitment. Eventually, Rebecca joined me at Lawton High. That's when the cracks began to show.

It happened on another trip to the movies. It was September, and we had tickets to some Nicolas Cage flick that absolutely no one wanted to see, a conscious decision on our part. We wanted the place to ourselves. She was wearing an electric-blue halter top, uncharacteristic for her. She seemed nervous. "Hey," she said, as if embarrassed by making her intentions so bare. "Uh . . . excited for Nic Cage?" It was perhaps the least sexually stimulating sentence I'd ever heard.

"Yes! Totally," I said. "Let's do it. I mean, yeah. Let's go."

To spare you the details, Wasted, we didn't have sex that day. We mostly fumbled around in the dark, blindly attempting to stimulate each other's nether regions. It was during that movie that an existential crisis began to unfold in me: I couldn't do this. I could try and try and try, and all I would ever be able to do was try while never quite getting "there." And was that any way to live? Was that really fair to Rebecca?

A gulf widened between us, a gulf that was wide enough for James to enter the picture. Tall and lanky with his hair greased back and a single stud in one ear, James was like something out of S. E. Hinton's *The Outsiders*. He always smelled like cigarette smoke and walked with a delinquent gait. Rebecca would end up cheating on me with him at the mall.

"Aren't you and Rebecca still together?" a text from one of my friends asked.

"Yeah," I replied. "Why?"

I received a blurry photo of her and James holding hands (Motorola Razr days). I fell back onto the couch. My first instinct was that of profound betrayal: how could someone I cared so much about do this to me? But then, I knew exactly how.

Over the past few weeks, I hadn't been paying her much attention at all. I was afraid, Wasted, which isn't an excuse but it's at least an explanation. I wasn't being a good boyfriend, and her friends surely had started to ask her why she was still with me.

After she was found out, she called me up.

"I'm so sorry," she opened, her voice already hoarse from crying. "It's just . . . I don't know, man. I'm sorry."

"Rebecca," I said, "I . . ." My first instinct was to make her feel better. That had been the instinct that had first brought us together. But I felt, this time, that I was the one who had hurt her.

By this time, a lot had changed in my life. I was rail thin, for one, thanks to a nascent eating disorder. I had made a group of friends, and I was engaging in a strategy around my homosexuality that involved not thinking about sex of any kind. I had acquired a kind of coldness, a "switching off" of my informant characteristics that I thought were betraying me too often—anything swishy, anything "too much."

"I'm sorry too," I said, and had almost said "I'm *sorrier*" but kept it down. It was true, though.

Rebecca and I retained an amicable distance after that, but the lessons of our relationship only grew more cumbersome to wrestle with as I slowly but surely came into a better understanding of myself.

What was that about?

It's hard, if not altogether impossible, for me to imagine a youth in which I was allowed to be gay. Or rather, a youth in which I was just allowed to *be*, to wallow in that fruitful messiness of early teendom without all the restrictions I'd placed on myself, to share my first kiss, to experience puppy love, to do everything I did with Rebecca, only, with a boy. It's easy to think of those years, Wasted, as an adolescence lost, precious time that was stolen from me.

But that's not quite right—I *did* experience those things, with Rebecca. And while, yes, it would have been nice to have experienced them with a boy like in some kind of progressive, gay young-adult-book-turned-movie, I do cherish the time I had with Rebecca. I cherish all of it—the infatuation and the frustration and the drifting apart. So much of our formative years are spent on building ourselves against opposition, navigating social restrictions and taboos, looking for our reflection in the devil's water before cautiously dipping our feet in and wondering, *Is this what I like? Is this who I am?*

I navigated that fraught process with Rebecca, who was, at worst, just a friend. In a way, I couldn't have been luckier.

I've entertained the notion that I might be bisexual, Wasted. I'd be silly not to have. The conclusion I've reached is that, yes, there are very specific circumstances in which I could see myself enjoying physical or romantic stimulation with a woman, but I've yet to see those circumstances materialize or have that situation actually occur. I remain open to challenges to my perception of my sexuality and to my reading on my desires, and as we as a collective continue to shift the vocabulary around sexual orientation and identity, I imagine that self-understanding will change. Or at the very least, my vocabulary for it will. It already has in some ways, with words like "queer" waxing and waning in popularity.

Seeing it that way, Wasted, has helped take the weight of my "lost years" off my shoulders. In so many ways, I am still trying to figure myself out, trying to crudely map the fugitive psychological landscape of my likes and dislikes, my affinities and revulsions. What if "coming out of the closet" didn't herald the beginning of an entirely new life, an event that partitioned my life into a BC and AD?

What if, Wasted, I'm still not so different from that kid who was chasing after someone, anyone, who would validate his place in the world and make him feel less alone? What if I'm still navigating taboos and social expectations and making missteps along the way? I think I prefer that way of looking at it, because I find myself wanting to "keep" the time I spent with Rebecca. I don't want to see our relationship as a failed experiment or a sad attempt at hiding who I really was. I want to include that time, the good and the bad, in the project of my life. I want to be happy when I think of the times Rebecca made me happy. Perhaps, Wasted, that's my way of making peace.

Don't get me wrong. I think coming out is an important life event, and I want so very, very badly for young people to have the freedom to be themselves and to worry less about being bullied half to death like I was.

But I'm not willing to see any part of my past, or Rebecca, as disposable, as I think a lot of gay men do with prolific concepts like "gold star gay" (a gay man who's never had sex with a woman) or a performative disgust for vaginas (vuh-guy-nas). I think we sometimes reduce women, diminish women, cast women and their bodies as jokes or as failed attempts on our sexual liberty because we think that's a small revenge on the straightness that was unjustly imposed on us. I find that impulse somewhat under-standable but its manifestations lazy at best.

The truth, as always, is complicated. But at times I like to return to those late nights when I was in high school, phone between my shoulder and cheek, sleepily talking to Rebecca while playing *Halo*, when loving this person who'd fallen into my life felt like the easiest thing in the world. At the time, it was.

¡Hola Papi!

*How do I overcome my imposter syndrome
to live my life as an authentic Latino?*

*Signed,
Panicked Hispanic*

How to Be a Real Mexican

I took the job at Rosa's Tortilla Factory because I felt I wasn't Mexican enough. It was not, as I claimed, because I needed the money, dear Panicked. Nor was it because I absolutely *had* to put the experience on my college applications, a process I had recently begun as I prepared to enter my senior year of high school. It was entirely because of an abrupt realization that I was, in fact, a big fat fraud.

"Mijo!" my abuela called to me from the living room one afternoon, foiling my attempt to sneak out the front door in my uniform. "Come 'eeeeere."

I rolled my eyes and slid off my official Rosa's cap, as if not wearing it would make Abuela's disapproval of my job there any less severe. I should have known better. Abuela, she could sense shame a mile away. I think it was what sustained her, like food does for normal people. "Coming!" I replied.

She was on the couch watching her telenovelas, which we would sometimes watch together. She liked pointing to various characters on the screen and telling me she wanted to murder them. "That there is Carmen," she'd say, nodding to a pretty, pale lady in a short dress. "I would love to kill her." She'd mime strangulation with her hands. "I would kill her like this."

Abuela was a very short, very brown woman. She had an equally short, equally brown husband, Abuelo, whom she called "Chums." Chums had served in a war. It was unclear which war, as he so frequently changed the story. He liked to set up military reenactments for us on the kitchen table using the salt and pepper shakers and napkins to represent enemy troops. "See this?" he'd say, holding up the pepper shaker. "The Soviets." He'd then pick up the saltshaker. "This?" he'd say. "The KKK."

Chums had come back from the war with all these new slang words, and "chum" had been among them. Abuela immediately fell in love with the word because it adequately captured both the apathy and the grueling familiarity she felt for her husband. Chum. Chummy. Chums. "That there is just my chum, mijo."

"Mijo," she said now as the show cut to commercial, "I want to see you. I'll be dead soon." Abuela had been saying she would die soon for years, with diminishing impact.

"I'm right here," I said, standing in front of her in my uniform, a red Rosa's-branded polo and black slacks. I held my black cap in my hands, anxiously fingering the red rose stitched on the front.

She had a chunky knit shawl over her shoulders and wore her favorite sweatshirt, a gray fleece that said AMERICA on it in blocky navy letters. She squinted at me through her glasses and sucked her teeth, something she always did before talking shit. "Whatcha doing, huh?"

"I am going to work, Abuela," I said plainly.

"What do you do?" she asked, just to hear me say it.

"I work at the tortilla factory down the road," I said.

She paused, and then she cackled. Abuela had this cackle that sounded like she'd just caught the world in the middle of trying to play an elaborate trick on her and she was getting the last laugh. "Shoot for the moon, mijo," she said. "You'll land among the stars."

It was the reaction I'd expected from Abuela. It's not that it was out of the norm for a high school student to have a summer job, Panicked. It was just that *this* job, working in a Mexican restaurant, was a particular affront. I was deliberately undermining all the hard work Abuela had put into making me white.

The thing about my family, Panicked, is that we're Mexican, but not really. My mom is a brown woman from Texas and my dad is a white man from Oklahoma. My last name is "Brammer," which isn't exactly exotic. I grew up in rural Oklahoma, where my abuelos and my mom were the only Mexicans around. Evidence of this: my mother was voted "Most Likely to Run a Taco Stand" in her school newspaper. And we weren't just some of the only Mexicans around. We were some of the only *people* around, period. Our closest neighbors were cows, and they weren't terribly talkative.

My abuelos' families were from Chihuahua, where people shot each other for fun, or so I'd been told. But I'd never been. The only places in Mexico I'd visited were Cancún and Puerto Vallarta. I'd learned Spanish in a classroom, just enough to satisfy my foreign language requirement and, I suppose, to ask a policeman where the discotheque was. When I asked my mom why she hadn't raised me with Spanish, she'd said, as if it were obvious, "Who would I talk to?"

Abuela had been the architect of all this. All three of her kids, my mom, my uncle, and my aunt, had married white people. She'd grown up poor in a Texas barrio, the youngest of eleven kids, and she'd dropped out of the fourth grade to pick fruit for money. She'd struggled with English, so she didn't see the need for her children to bother with Spanish. By all accounts, she wasn't exactly a loving mother. But she hadn't wanted her kids to deal with the things she'd dealt with. I suppose that's what love was to her.

The result, Panicked? We all lost Spanish. We lost Christmas tamales. We lost quinceañeras, and we lost the sense that we were from somewhere else, that immutable otherness that separated my abuelos from me—their accents; the way they dressed; the color of their skin; their burdens. My mom, my sister, and I, meanwhile, were Americans with a squeeze of lime.

This was fine, inasmuch as it was all I knew, until one day I felt a sense of imposter syndrome I could no longer ignore. I was watching the news with Abuela on the couch; a bunch of bodies had just been discovered, buried under the border, murdered people. Mexicans were the enemy du jour then, in 2008. People were always on the news popping off about "illegals," about having to dial 1 for English.

"*Shee*," Abuela said to me, another favorite term of hers. I never figured out if she was shortening the word "shit" or mispronouncing "gee." She nudged me. "They sure do hate us, huh?" It was a jarring realization—*Oh, I am not unlike these widely disliked people.*

Don't get me wrong. It had occasionally occurred to me in life that I was a Mexican, Panicked. The middle school kids had called me "beaner" before. When I had told them (very matter-of-factly) that, actually, I was half German, they'd simply changed "beaner" into "beanerschnitzel," a pretty devastating portmanteau that spread like wildfire. It's probably what I deserved for lying about being half German. I'm not even sure what kind of white my dad is.

Those unfortunate incidents aside, I had always been Mexican in isolation. It was sort of like a fun fact, trivia. I had never put my identity in the context of a broader conversation. There was no "us," no "we" to it. But in that moment on the couch, Abuela connected me to something: me to her, us to *them*, we to some collective suffering. It disturbed me, because I felt no right to stand in it, but at the same time, I felt an obligation. I felt, suddenly, like a word missing its sentence.

So I took a job at the tortilla factory, one with a silly uniform and that Abuela didn't approve of.

"Thank you for believing in me," I said to her that afternoon, fake approval being about as good as it was going to get with her. I bent down and hugged her. "They might even let me work the cash register once I learn how to do math," I said in her ear.

"Bah," Abuela said, waving me off.

I hopped into my car, an old Mitsubishi Eclipse with a Mexican flag on the front license plate (I was very serious about this "becoming Mexican" business), and drove into town to Rosa's, listening to an eclectic mix of Vicente Fernández and reggaeton as I went. I sang along as best I could. Some lyrics I knew by memory, even if I didn't know what they actually meant. I sounded them out, recited them, knew them by their spirit.

Rosa's was painted pink, made to look like a hacienda. The inside was decorated with Talavera tiles, fake parrots hanging from the ceiling, and bullfighting posters on the walls. On my first day my new boss, a short, middle-aged man who went by Sly, showed me around.

"This is where Sal works," Sly said, showing me the sink. "Mean dude. He'll stab you for looking at him wrong. No mames." He'd grabbed a knife from the sink and made like he was going to stab me. He laughed, then I laughed, but I was shrieking inside.

It reminded me that my greatest hurdle in becoming Mexican was that I was soft. From what I'd gathered on TV and from my abuelos, being Mexican was mostly about suffering. It was about doing jobs no one else wanted to do. It was about getting called names, being poor, being blamed for everything, and then persevering anyway. It was about pain, and I had not experienced near enough pain, or at least not the kind Abuela had. I was an AP student who'd grown up with air-conditioning and who rarely went outside. "Spoiled," Abuela frequently spat at me. "You're spoiled rotten." I was desperate to correct that. But damn, Panicked. Did I have to get stabbed?

I didn't see much of Sal my first week. I mostly made tortillas. There was a part of the kitchen behind Plexiglas that people in the dining area could see into. There was a machine there that churned out the tortillas. I'd mix hot water and heaping cups of flour for the dough. I'd tear off chunks of it to roll into balls and feed them one by one into the machine.

Tortillas would file down the conveyer belt, warm, fluffy white clouds gathering in a basket at the bottom. Sometimes I'd get into the rhythm of it and dissociate. I'd imagine myself as a worker in heaven on a construction line, pumping out dreams to pass the time.

Sometimes kids would come up to the window, and I'd toss them a fresh tortilla through a slit in the Plexiglas like a Frisbee, or I'd give them a little bit of dough to play with. It was dull, repetitive work. But my coworkers made it interesting.

The first time I saw Javier, Sal, and Rodrigo, they were posted up on the kitchen table, mean-mugging me like I'd stolen something. Other people worked there, and some employees floated in and then out, but I remember those three the best, because they talked to me the most.

Javier and Rodrigo were short, stocky men, middle-aged and covered in tattoos. Javier wore a gold watch, and Rodrigo had a massive scar on his cheek. Sal was a tank, six foot something, with a pouf of coarse, wiry hair trying to spring his cap off his head. With weak knees I said, "Hola," like an idiot. The word felt insulting leaving my mouth.

They glared at me for what felt like several minutes before breaking character and shouting, in unison, "*AYYY!*" There was a flurry of questions. Where you from? You Mexican? What's your name? You speak Spanish?

I'm from here. My mom is. John Paul. Un poquito.

"Paisano!" Javier shouted, slapping me on the back so hard I thought my eyeballs were going to shoot out of my skull. "Countryman," a word I'd heard from Abuelo before. I felt a sharp stab of anxiety: *Please, Lady of Guadalupe above, don't let them test my Spanish.*

Of course they decided to test my Spanish. They asked me things about girls and school and life. And I failed spectacularly, what little Spanish I did know flying out of my brain like startled pigeons. But to my surprise, their response to my poor Spanish wasn't to chastise me. It was to teach me.

"We will talk shit about you to your face," Javier explained. "When you get mad, we will know you learned." It wasn't exactly Rosetta Stone, but it proved effective.

I studied up on Spanish in my spare time, curious as to what heinous things the gang was saying about me. Javier and Rodrigo called me a colorful assortment of names—pinche pendejo, puto, flaco, pinche guey—intermingled with sentences I actually needed to learn. *When do you get off work? What do you like to do? Can you help me with this?*

It wasn't entirely a charity. It was more of an exchange. My coworkers, in turn, wanted me to teach them English words. Specifically, they wanted to know how to say "dick" in as many different ways as possible. English, as with any language worth its salt, is host to a breathtaking diversity of ways to say "penis." "Cock," "tool," "wang," "knob," "dong," "trouser snake"; I taught them all of it. I even taught them "dick"-adjacent words like "dildo" and "chode."

Their favorite, however, was far and away "prick." I had struggled to transition out of Spanish-speaking mode when I first said it, and I had accidentally rolled my *r* on it. "Prrrrrrríck," I'd said, which sent them into hysterics.

"Prrrrríck!" Rodrigo said to me, and he said it like it was a French delicacy, like he was a world-renowned gourmet chef announcing his next dish.

"Prrrríck," I'd say, nodding at Javier, and the title would move around throughout the workday like a game of hot potato until someone gave up. It was usually me.

I became especially close to Javier, who took a liking to me after I told him my family was from Chihuahua, a partial truth based in ignorance. I'd seen the old newspaper clipping about my abuela's family coming over in a wagon. It was in an obituary for some family member I'd never met. I used to imagine Abuela in the wide barrel of a covered wagon, sitting among Ellis Island–style trunks. It probably looked nothing like that, but the idea of Abuela's being ancient enough to have come over in a wagon like she was on some kind of Mexican Oregon Trail was funny to me.

Javier was from Juárez. He—like Rodrigo, like Sal—was undocumented. He had a gold tooth, a fact I didn't discover until I started being around him up close more often. He had two daughters, Eva and Marisol, and he was trying to keep them in school. They were embarrassed by him, he told me once, because he was a part-time janitor at their school. I thought that was a heavy thing to admit, but Javier laughed like he was playing a joke on them by doing it. He'd finish his shift there, and then he'd come here.

I had my first beer ever with Javier at the ripe old age of seventeen. He took me to the freezer with Tecate and we toasted "to the hustle." He called me Juan Pablo instead of John Paul, which he later shortened to Juanpa, which sounded like "wompa" to me, but I didn't protest—I liked it. It made me into someone else.

Javier taught me how to make Mexican food. Off the books, of course, since I didn't have a food handler's license. I made enchiladas and tacos and learned how to properly stuff and roll a snug burrito. I fried sopapillas and diced up tomatoes for salsa, and every time I did something right Javier would slap me on the back and say, "You a real Mexican now."

I was embarrassed by how badly I wanted his approval and by how good it felt when I got it. I felt I was using him. It wasn't his job. He was a person, not a translator, not a "study abroad" experience. But still, I saw him as someone who could validate me, someone who could make me real. And, Panicked, I desperately wanted to be real.

I continued my summer job at Rosa's into the school year. My classmates were bitterly divided over the 2008 presidential election that was shaping up for November. My school was majority Black, but it was still Oklahoma. Every day there were racist jokes—jokes about lynching, about how Black people shouldn't be allowed to vote.

A racist tide raises all racist ships, I suppose. These Black "jokes" opened the floodgates for Mexican jokes as well, and it was frightening to see so many people, people I thought I knew, showing their true colors by making them. Jokes about "sending the beaners back," jokes about wetbacks, about spics. I felt angry every day. But it was an anger I still felt I had no right to.

That spring, when I was admitted to Duke University and a classmate said I had only been let in because I was Mexican, I admit my first reaction was to feel validated. I felt maybe I was Mexican after all. Maybe I wasn't a fake, and maybe that meant

I did belong in my own skin, because I felt pain, affirming pain, pain that would make me real if I got enough of it.

But the feeling of fraudulence would creep back in, and I would be back in that place where I was angry but had no language to address that anger. I felt someone had stolen it from me. But who? I felt least angry around Javier, who called me terrible names in Spanish and who made me feel welcome in myself.

I gleaned some hints as to how Javier saw me. Once, I had brought a college application to fill out during the lulls at work. It was for Stanford.

"Damn, guey," Javier said, leaning over the table, close enough to see the salsa I'd spilled on the immaculate campus ad. He was invested in my college application process, always asking me how it was going, where I was applying. "I didn't know you was smart like that."

"It's true, I'm a genius," I told Javier. "I'm going to Stanford to become a nuclear physicist or some shit."

A new employee, Jessie, was passing through the kitchen on her way to the tables. She was tall with black hair, skinny and with a permanent air of irritation about her that kept her nose up all the time. Passing through, she craned over into our conversation. "Shouldn't you be working in construction?" she said casually. It was meant to be a joke—the crux of which was that I was a Mexican. It could have been harmful, but instead I took it as validation that she thought of me as a Mexican.

Javier didn't feel that way. He shot up from the kitchen table, moving with the surprising speed of a crocodile jolted into action. He chased Jessie out into the dining area. "Yo!" he said with vehemence I hadn't heard before, and I immediately thought of his daughters, two people who would recognize this other voice. "Take that shit back!"

I retreated to the bathroom to avoid their bickering, not because I hated conflict—which I did—but because I felt guilt. I *was* guilty, Panicked. What I was doing was wrong.

Who was I to want anything from Javier? Javier was dealing with real problems. Javier was out there defending me (of all people) while he was undocumented, while he was struggling to support his kids, while he was trying to learn English. He wasn't there as part of some validating cultural activity. He was there for his survival.

The things I wanted for myself, the things I thought would make me "real"—a Mexican last name, Mexican customs and traditions and language—these were things that made Javier's life harder in ways I had never known. Jessie's flippantly telling me to work construction was mean. But it had no power over me. It existed only on the plane of rhetoric, where the two of us were on an even playing field. It wouldn't hold me back, and so it bounced right off me. But it stuck for Javier. It meant something to Javier.

Weeks went by, smelling of old salsa and queso, as school continued to pick up. I had become the president of, like, four different clubs, mostly because I had been the only one to raise my hand. I was the Spanish club president, the president of the National Honor Society, and the editor in chief of the yearbook, and yet I hardly did anything because our school was mostly interested in not getting shut down by the government and avoiding hallway stabbings.

I started bringing books and homework to the restaurant, and Javier would ask to take a look at them. "You should quit," he told me once, leafing through my math book. "You suck at this job."

But before I would inevitably quit, I had my final Spanish exam. It took the form of a disgruntled customer whom Rodrigo and Javier giddily pushed me into dealing with.

The customer was a short, slim woman in a halter top who wore her sunglasses indoors and had long acrylic nails. She marched her plastic tray up to the register and slammed it down.

"No English, her," Rodrigo said, grinning ear to ear. "Go ahead."

"Fine," I sighed. I walked up to the counter, ready to face the final boss battle of my video game. The woman looked at me, and although I couldn't see her eyes, I could tell she was ready to behead me.

"Hola," I said to her. "Qué es tu problema?"

I wasn't exactly sure what she said back, but it sounded like she was methodically cursing out my ancestors one by one, plucking them individually from the branches of my family tree, generation by generation, before arriving at me.

I did manage to pick up, however, that she'd wanted chicken tacos instead of beef.

"Lo siento," I said again and again in my dumb gringo accent. "Voy a . . . make . . . tacos nuevos." I heard Rodrigo and Javier busting a gut in the kitchen. "Un minuto, por favor."

I went back to the kitchen; punched Javier and Rodrigo, which only made them laugh harder; and made the chicken tacos. The woman, meanwhile, was still talking without me there, fighting the very memory of me. I sheepishly returned with her food. I meant to tell her they were on the house, that they were free. What I actually said, according to Javier's subsequent translation, was "Freedom tacos."

"Here," I'd said. "Freedom tacos."

The woman, perhaps so thrown off by this that she perceived it as a power move, accepted the new tacos and went back to her table. Rodrigo and Javier practically jumped on me, applauding me and laughing so hard I thought they might fall over. For a moment, I stopped taking myself so seriously. I had utterly failed. I was having a great time.

At last, my final day in the tortilla factory came. I was asked to do the most unpleasant tasks in the restaurant as a farewell gift. I walked into the sticky room where the bladders of soda were kept for the pop machine and I cleaned the floor. I cleaned the bathrooms and then the tables. But the worst task was carrying a vat of hot grease out to the dumpster.

Javier helped me with this, yellow grease lapping up at the lip of the vat as we walked, threatening to spill over with each step. "Ten cuidado, Juanpa," he told me.

I watched the snake god tattooed on his arm. It wriggled as he strained, its body covered in feathers, ancient and fierce.

It was my second-favorite tattoo of his. The other was the enormous Our Lady of Guadalupe he had on his back. She'd made a less than miraculous appearance once in the kitchen, when Sal had accused Javier of being a dirty bastard. Javier had lifted up his shirt, turned around, and said, "Say it to her!"

I was thinking how funny it was that these two competing

gods could find a common place on Javier's body when my foot caught on a crack in the concrete. I stumbled a little, enough to spill some hot grease on Javier's arm. "SHIT!" he shouted.

We quickly set the vat down and retreated into the shade of the building, where we sat in the grass, Javier hissing into his arm, my heart racing a mile a minute as I said, over and over, the one stupid phrase I could rely on: "Lo siento. Lo siento. Lo siento. Lo siento."

Lo siento.

I still say that to Abuela sometimes in my head, hoping it will reach her wherever she is, be it heaven or hell or somewhere else. It's probably hell. I feel I want to apologize to her, like I apologized to Javier, for using her pain to validate my identity. I used to resent the fact that she didn't teach me Spanish, that she didn't maintain our family traditions. I have come to understand that her decision to ditch those things was more "authentically Mexican" than performing any of the rituals I thought of as real—listening to reggaeton, making tacos, caring about a flag.

Lo siento.

I didn't realize how intrinsically American it was of me to think I could "have" an identity by "having" things—Spanish, tattoos, silver chains, scars. If I could do it again, Panicked, I would tell myself that identity is defined as much by what you have as it is by what you've lost. Wanting to recover those things was like feeling homesick for a home I never had. That, to me, is Chicano.

Lo siento.

I've come to understand, Panicked, that race is a lie. But it's a lie like money is a lie, which means it's real, because it's a system. You can't really opt out of it. You have to play along with it to some degree, which, I've realized, was the source of my youthful anger: I went from being "American," unencumbered by identity, to realizing that I had in fact been burdened, tasked with something, and I blamed everyone around me for it. I blamed my "authentically" Mexican family for putting me in that situation by not preparing me, by not telling me what I was and allowing the world to surprise me with it instead. I blamed myself, too, because who was I, surrounded by all the comforts they had sacrificed to give me, to tell them they were wrong?

Lo siento.

The answer is: I'm no one at all, except for my experiences. I am the things I've seen and the things I've felt. I am the people I've met. Those things are authentic. You can't lie your way in or out of them like you can lie your way into a college, like you can lie to your white friends about whether or not the Mexican restaurant you're eating at is "real," just to feel a temporary surge in authority, in authenticity. All that is to say, Panicked, it's not about whether you can make tacos or not. It helps, but it's not about that. Race is a system more concerned with creating experiential differences than it is about whether or not you're "really" anything. Abuela and Javier taught me that. It's more important that you care about the lives and the pain of the people around you than it is for you to know how to say "dick" in Spanish. It's more important that you listen rather than speak.

"Lo siento," I said again in the shadow of the Rosa's building, as if the hundredth time would undo what I had done to Javier.

Javier sucked his teeth. He pulled a cigarette from his pocket, lit it, and took a long drag. He exhaled and turned his other arm, the one that hadn't just been burned, to show me. "Look," he said, and I saw several scars and grease burns. This must have happened to him plenty of times before. My arms, meanwhile, had never felt so clean and unused.

"I'm sorry," I said in English.

"You know what you are?" he said, locking eyes with me, his face deathly serious, my heart leaping.

"What?" I asked.

"A prrrríck," he said.

I let out a cackle, relief and joy and sadness. I thought it sounded an awful lot like my abuela's.

¡Hola Papi!

How do I let go of a rotten relationship?

Signed,
Addicted to You

How to Come Out to Your Boyfriend
in a Walmart Parking Lot

There were three things I didn't want to admit about Corey and me, Addicted.

First, I didn't want to admit that there might have been something gay about the two of us seizing on every opportunity to jerk each other off. Whenever we were alone, be it in my apartment when he visited me in Norman, where I was attending the University of Oklahoma, or in his room when I went home to visit him in Lawton, the door would barely have time to close before our pants dropped. It's not that you *have* to be gay to jerk another guy off, mind you. But in my case, I was doing some serious mental gymnastics to convince myself that getting naked with my "best friend" from high school was just two hetero bros doing regular hetero-bro stuff.

Luckily, like many closeted gay men, I was an adept mental gymnast. Here's an example: one time I was at a Lady Gaga concert and she asked if there were any straight men in the room, any

71

straight men at all, and I was among the dozen or so who clapped. Cognitive dissonance is an old friend of mine.

The second thing I didn't want to admit about Corey and me was that I was in love with him. That might sound an awful lot like the first thing, and sure, there might have been something "gay" about my being "in love with a man." But I had dreamed up a perfectly reasonable scenario wherein I could love Corey and not be gay: We would simply follow each other around for the rest of our natural lives and avoid the subject of gayness altogether. We'd move into neighboring houses, houses full of empty rooms with doors that locked, and I'd survive on scraps—discreet hand jobs, road trips, the rare moments of tenderness he showed me sometimes, whispers of "I love you, man" and gentle pats on my head, always when no one was around. We'd both die at some point, and then I wouldn't have to worry about it anymore.

All that is to say, Addicted, that I could work around being in love with Corey. It was more that I *resented* being in love with him. I felt he had played some elaborate trick on me while I wasn't looking. Rolling down the streets of Lawton on a clear summer night in his old Grand Cherokee, as we had done hundreds of times before, I played a little game. I looked at him, his wrist on the steering wheel, his eyes squinting diligently ahead, toothpick flicking around in his mouth, and I imagined him as a stranger with whom I had no history.

I asked myself why I should be in love with this person. Was it that he was handsome? No, not really. Sure, Corey had that whole dumb jock thing going for him that some idiots (me) were into, but I'd seen dumber and jockier. He was dishwater blond and husky with brown eyes and an apathetic slouch in his back. He'd been a baseball player in high school, but he'd sucked at it so bad that I didn't factor it into his final score. Realistically, I could have found another Corey walking around the local mall if I tried.

Nevertheless, I loved him, a fact that I couldn't square with anything else—unjustifiable, unacceptable, but a fact.

The third and final thing I couldn't admit about Corey and me was that we desperately needed to part ways. Our relationship had been ruined long ago, and staying in it was eating away at our lives. But truth be told, try as I might, I couldn't imagine my life without him.

I had just wrapped up my sophomore year in college and had only recently decided it was about time to come out of the closet. It wasn't an easy decision. I'm not sure I would have come out that year if I hadn't taken an Adderall to keep me awake for my biology final a few weeks prior, hyping me up so much that, in a fit of gay mania, I started Facebook messaging everyone I knew revealing that I was a homosexual. Responses ran the gamut from "I support you" to "Yeah, I figured" to "That's cool, man, but do I know you?" Telling a dozen or so people helped me work up the courage to admit it to myself.

"Where do you want to go?" Corey asked me that night as we drove around.

"There's always Walmart," I offered. In our small city of Lawton, Walmart was the de facto center of the universe. This was before we got higher-end options, like Target. We would wander the aisles, browse the electronics, flirt with theft, and pick up unnecessary baked goods—a birthday cake, maybe, or apple turn-overs, or muffins, to be devoured in indulgent fits of spontaneity.

"Walmart," Corey agreed. There was something solemn and final about the way he said it, as if he knew I had decided to press the nuclear button, that I had decided to come out to him that night, and he was bracing for impact. I didn't doubt that he knew. Four years of nonstop contact with someone can give you that kind of sixth sense. Or maybe it was the hand jobs.

As he steered us down the empty streets, I was still playing my little game, imagining him as someone I'd never met. It made him mystical, in a way. It made me wonder how things between two people could get so messed up, how a person could go from being no one in particular to being Corey.

I'd first met Corey back when he'd tried to convert me to his Christian youth cult our junior year in high school. We'd been assigned desks right next to each other in first period, and I remember dreading having to fend off his attempts to "save" me. Corey had a reputation back then. I'd describe him as an ideal pro-tagonist for a faith-based film with a Christian-rock soundtrack—he was from a rough neighborhood, got in fights all the time, and was flunking out of everything before he found Jesus.

Meanwhile, I was taking confirmation classes at my local Catholic church to appease my Mexican mother. These were the expedited classes frequented by old people who were at death's door and needed to get a move on. "The lightning round," I called it. Two people died within my first few weeks of class, which was held in the stuffy rec center at Holy Family. "Survival of the fittest," my mother would tell me when dropping me off.

The very first day Corey sat down next to me, he did exactly what I'd expected him to do. "Hey, man," he said, low and apologetic, the way evangelicals talk when they first approach you, out of respect for your heathen ignorance. "I was just wondering what your relationship with Jesus is like."

"He's ignoring my texts," I said. In my mind, I was an exceptionally clever young adult. "Why, what has he told you?"

He smiled. "You don't have to be disrespectful," he said. He was wearing a black band tee and skinny jeans that were much too tight. It was the unofficial uniform of FUEL. Not an acronym for anything. It was just spelled in all capital letters for emphasis. Their logo was a skater boy performing a sick jump over a raging fire. They called their organization a "youth group," but to people outside of it, it seemed like a cult.

I'm not calling it a cult because I have an axe to grind with Christianity or anything. FUEL placed a high premium on skateboarding and pizza to obscure the fact that they were primarily concerned with beating demons out of people. That's not a metaphor. They thought they could punch Satan out of you with their fists. I'd seen the videos on Facebook. They would beat the shit out of each other between Hillsong sets.

"Well, you asked," I said before turning away from him.

"Man," he said. He seemed amused, like the game was officially afoot and I had proven to be an especially clever species of prey, like he was a lion and I was a gazelle with a jet pack. "So it's gonna be like that, huh?"

In my mind, there was no dialogue to have. FUEL's student members were notoriously impossible. They would protest in biology class whenever Mr. Adams, our extremely bald and jaded science teacher, presented anything about evolution. They would stand up with their arms firmly clapped at their sides, a defiant look plastered on their faces to signal to God that they were having no part of this, that they objected to the funny business of fish developing limbs.

"All right, man," Corey said. "I'll leave you alone."

Addicted, he did not leave me alone.

Day after day, he pestered me to have a conversation with him about God, and day after day, I thwarted him, getting progressively ruder about it as I went. Weeks flew by, and his attempts persisted.

I was in a world religions class at the time—a new elective that I viewed as an easy A—where our teacher, Ms. Cloutier, who also taught French, would describe the religions to us in her detached way, her thick accent making her sound all the more disinterested, as if the faiths of the world were different kinds of fish in a tank and not, as it were, cosmic truths. She once told us a parable—I think it was Hindu—about an eagle holding a feather that would fly over a mountain once a year and brush its tip with the feather. Over hundreds of thousands of years, the eagle would at last reduce the mountain to nothing, bringing about the end of the world and the start of a new era.

The story frightened me because I immediately thought of Corey. The idea of fending him off from the mountaintop of my life until school ended seemed exhausting and rote. I eventually relented. "Let's just have lunch," he said one afternoon. "We don't even have to talk about FUEL."

Hindsight being 20/20, I probably shouldn't have agreed. But here we are, Addicted—the sum of our choices, the gas station hot dogs we decide to eat with Corey. I climbed into his Grand Cherokee and we drove to the duck pond five minutes from campus to chat. I admit, as someone without a car at the time, it felt like an exclusive experience to leave the cafeteria behind, a rush of adult mischief that I found altogether enjoyable.

"So," he said, his eyes on the steering wheel. He was suddenly sheepish, his holy fire nowhere to be found. I might have guessed why. All his badgering to get me to go to lunch with him, now that it had finally happened, seemed uncomfortably like courtship. We were two dudes eating hot dogs by a duck pond. Alone. And it had been completely his idea. "I guess . . . Uh . . ."

As much as I enjoyed watching him squirm, I, too, felt embarrassed. I thought maybe we should talk about religion after all. It was something to do, at least. Besides, I wanted to ask Corey if he really thought a youth pastor with frosted tips and cargo shorts had happened upon the meaning of life. "Shit," I said. "Let's get it over with."

"Can you not cuss in front of me?" he asked, so earnestly it startled me. "Please?"

"Why?" I asked.

"Because I don't like obscenity."

"I'll stop if you can spell 'obscenity.'"

"No."

"Fine, I won't cuss."

Corey fidgeted in his seat. I imagined he was preparing to deliver the spiel he'd given to dozens of other unfortunate souls. A few other FUEL kids had already given it to me. They would ask about God, and then they would tell me about what a drag hell would be, and then they'd invite me to the FUEL warehouse downtown.

"I was just wondering if, like, you had any questions."

"Questions?" I said.

"Yeah."

"Not really."

"Everyone has questions," he said. "Even I have questions."

"Wow," I said in mock admiration. "Even you?"

He sighed. "That's not what I mean."

"Then what do you mean?"

"Man," he said, that sly grin on his face that made it seem like he thought of this, *all* of this, as a game, God included. It confused me, because I thought he took the business of saving people very seriously. But he enjoyed it when I rebuffed him, like it was his preference. "If you would just come to FUEL with me one time . . ."

"I would rather eat my left nut for breakfast," I said.

"Dude, obscenity . . ."

"I said 'nut'!"

"Still."

"Okay, sorry."

He stared through the windshield. "I just mean there's a lot I don't know," he said. "I don't have all the answers."

I felt bad. Sure, maybe he was trying to lure me into a warehouse to beat the actual devil out of me while my creepy class-mates played shitty Christian rap music for ambiance. But he wasn't lying about anything, and he was doing his best not to insult me while I was trying very hard to insult him. Guilty, I relented. "All right," I said. "I do have some questions."

My questions weren't as sophisticated as I thought; in retro-spect they were at an *Agnosticism for Dummies* level. But I asked them anyway. I asked Corey about people born into other reli-gions, about Hindus, Buddhists, Muslims, and everyone else. I asked him if he really believed they were all going to hell. I asked why, if God was so good, there was so much evil.

"I hear you," Corey said every time I finished, as if my ques-tions weren't questions but general statements. "I'm going to ask about that." A lot of it came down to mysteries. Corey said he didn't know some things, but that faith was about not knowing. He said he would get back to me with what his pastor said, and that we should get lunch again the next day.

To make a long story short, Addicted, I accidentally killed Corey's God in the duck pond parking lot over the course of several lunches. Though I think Corey was only hanging on to God by a thread to begin with. He needed something to give his chaotic life some sense of order, and FUEL had merely shown up before a biker gang or the military or literally anything else.

"Man," he told me one afternoon, a shit-eating grin on his face. "You won't believe what I said today at FUEL."

"What?" I asked. We were idling by the duck pond, which was entirely bereft of ducks as always, eating hot dogs.

"I asked how you could be pro-life and pro-war at the same

time," he told me, as if he expected me to reward him with a treat. "Like, how you gonna be against abortion but then kill a shit ton of people, you know what I mean? It don't make no sense, dude!"

As God's influence receded, curse words made a colorful return to Corey's vocabulary. He could hardly open his mouth without a few "fuck"s and "bitch"es flying out. Religion, meanwhile, was suddenly chock-full of contradictions. He took pride in plucking them out and showing them to me, like a cat dropping a dead bird on a porch as a kind of twisted gift. I was flattered.

He started taking pride in being my friend, too. His FUEL pals were warning him to stop being around me, as I was "disrupting his faith walk," which made me feel like an impossibly powerful demon. It felt like just being around each other made us rebels, beating the odds and breaking the rules. The reality was much less exciting. We were just two guys hanging out by a duck pond, talking about life. But that changed, too.

We started hanging out without God, after our journeys with religion came to their conclusions. I was confirmed in the Catholic Church (alongside the survivors of my class) with the saint name "Juan Diego," and Corey parted ways with FUEL, an experience he decided was hilarious in retrospect. He'd tell me stories about the exorcisms and about making up Hebrew words on the spot to make it seem like he'd been speaking in tongues. As God faded away, space opened up for us to get to know each other on a deeper level.

I learned that Corey came from a rough home. His mother, a squat, aggressively friendly woman, was the breadwinner. She worked as a secretary at a smoked meat corporation. His father, brooding and weathered, was a flooring guy who'd been hit hard by the 2008 recession. The old white handyman van loitered like a sad ornament outside their clapboard house in a potholed neighborhood in Lawton. In all the years I knew Corey, I never saw it move.

His house became like my house. We'd eat lunch together at school, meet up after the last class of the day, and go back to his place, where we'd play *Call of Duty* on his bed. His mom would make us dinner, and we'd pray his dad wouldn't be in one of his stormy moods. Sometimes he was, though, and Corey and I would go on miniature road trips through Lawton to escape. It was on those nights, cruising around town, bumping along the backcountry roads, that we revealed even more of ourselves to each other.

"Did you used to hate me?" he asked one night in his car. We thought it was fun to do that, to pick apart our origin story.

"Absolutely," I said. It was our senior year. We had ordered our robes and graduation caps. I would be headed to the University of Oklahoma, and he would be going "down the road," which is what we in Lawton called the local college. "I still do."

By that time, Addicted, I think Corey knew everything about me. He knew I was insecure about being mixed. He knew I didn't really like any of the girls in our class in a romantic way. He knew I got depressed sometimes, and he knew that I dreamed of becoming a writer. It wasn't that I told him these things directly—he seemed to absorb them through osmosis.

But things were going to change. I teased the idea of his coming to OU with me. He was a huge Sooner football fan, and he liked the thought of it, but he said his grades were too low and he didn't have the money. He said he would try, though, and that he'd come join me after the fall semester. Maybe we could live together. That calmed me down a bit. It was only about an hour and fifteen minutes away by car, but I couldn't shake the feeling that I was going to lose Corey, and in turn, a big chunk of myself.

It was the first time I'd ever been terrified of losing someone. It was through preparing to say goodbye that I started to realize what I actually felt for Corey wasn't just friendship, though I didn't really know what other kind of love it could possibly be.

In the middle of summer, he was supposed to drive to Florida with his parents for a family vacation for a whole week. At that point, it had been years since I'd gone a week without seeing Corey.

He'd just dropped me off at my house, as he'd done hundreds of times before. "Later, dude!" he called out to me as he threw his car in reverse. "Bring back an alligator!" I called back, and I waved him goodbye. I was barefoot, the concrete burning my soles. The cicadas were hissing as I watched Corey's face grow less and less distinct through the blue tint of his windshield until it disappeared altogether. My stomach dropped to my feet. I didn't want him to leave—that much, I could acknowledge. What I couldn't acknowledge was what I really wanted: for him to stay with me.

He occupied every corner of my brain while he was away. What was he doing? Was he thinking of me, too? I would consider texting him before realizing it had only been five minutes since I'd last done so. He uploaded one picture to Facebook the entire time, of himself in the back seat of his mom's van, smiling vacantly. I looked at it every day.

Everywhere I went, I imagined what being there with Corey

would be like, what he'd say, what he'd do. I became envious of the everyday things he was seeing without me. The beach. The Mexican restaurants. I was jealous of the ocean. It was miserable. *I* was miserable. My parents asked me what was wrong, why I wasn't eating. I had nothing to say.

I had no vocabulary for being in love with another man, Addicted. I had never let myself learn it for fear that I would have to use it one day.

When Corey came back from Florida, I clung to him and the few precious weeks we had left. I got nervous when I went too long without seeing him. He would try to talk to me about girls he liked, and I would shoot him down, dismissing them for one reason or another. Gabby was too promiscuous. Sarah was too demanding. Sabotage.

Corey had clearly been transformed, too.

"I love you, man," he said one night when we were driving through Norman. It seemed to come off the top of his head, a thought he hadn't considered too hard before letting it out.

"Well," I said. "I enjoy you . . . at times . . ."

He pushed my head a little, the brief warmth of his big catcher's-mitt hand on the back of my neck enough to send a bolt of excitement down my spine. "You're a jerk," he said.

His arm rested next to mine, so close that our fingers just grazed. I wondered if he was doing it on purpose.

I thought I was losing my mind, looking for little signs in everything he did—he'd run his fingers through my hair, then give me a shove; he'd rub my shoulders, then push me away. Every tender act was punctuated by a physical "no homo." Life was like that for a while, short spurts of bliss bookended by twists of the knife: *Maybe he feels the way I do*, but, oh, wait, *No he doesn't, of course he doesn't.*

On the worst of these nights, he invited me to housesit for his grandmother with him. Summer was ending, and I had made no progress in figuring out how I was going to move on while leaving him behind. Corey was standing in the driveway holding a carton of eggs.

"The hell are you doing?" I asked. He had that same old smirk on his face, plotting something devious.

"We're gonna egg someone's shit," he said, pleased with himself.

"We're not going to egg anyone's shit," I said. I'd never felt so old and stuffy as I did when I talked him down from egging random people's cars. "Put those back in the fridge."

"Damn, man," he said. "You're no fun, huh?"

It was jarring to realize the flip in our dynamic—Corey used to scold me for swearing, and now I was the one babysitting him.

There were doilies everywhere inside his grandmother's house, a glass case for creepy porcelain figurines, and a large bedroom with a bed covered in chunky quilts. "Well," he said, as if he blamed me for the dull nature of the house, as if I had conspired with it against him, "what are we gonna do instead?" I didn't have any bright ideas.

"We could play video games," I suggested.

He sighed, perhaps considering all the cars we could have egged by now if I weren't such a stick-in-the-mud. He picked up the Wii remote and tossed himself on the couch. I went to collect mine, annoyed that Corey was throwing a fit, and saw that a dog had chewed up the second Wii remote. There wasn't even a dog in the house.

"I'm not using this," I said, holding the gnarled remains at a repulsed distance.

"So I'm supposed to use it?" he said without looking at me.

"Yes," I said. "You are."

"Oh yeah?" he said. He looked at me and held the pristine remote by its wrist strap, swinging it tauntingly. He smiled. "Why don't you come take this one, then?"

An invitation we'd both been waiting for. I wrapped my arms around his waist and pulled us down to the ground. Corey tossed the remote aside and rolled over on top of me, his weight pinning me to the carpet.

"Say 'uncle,'" he said.

I writhed around, kicking my legs until at last I was able to throw him off me. I locked my legs with his and rolled him over. I buried my knee into his back, held his wrists down to the ground. "You say it," I said, panting, red faced. I knew he was bigger and stronger than me, but I was more determined.

He rose up, sending me lurching forward. I lost my grip on his wrists, and he knocked me down. We rolled around, over and then under each other, our faces mere inches apart. It was then that I realized that I was hard. I was wearing basketball shorts, as was my summer custom, and I was terrified he would notice.

I let him roll me onto my stomach, where I could hide my erection. He laid the entirety of himself on top of me, his mouth right next to my ear, so close I could feel him breathing on my cheek. "You give up?" he grunted. I felt it through his shorts. He was hard, too. His arousal was just as frightening as mine, if not more so. I felt, of all things, guilt. It was like I blamed myself for it, this thing I wanted so badly that shouldn't have been happening.

We stayed there for a while, him on top of me, both of us trying to catch our breath. But we didn't dare relax our bodies; doing so would be to admit the thing we couldn't admit. If he were to rest on top of me, it would mean he wanted to be there. If I were to stop pushing, it would mean I was enjoying this.

I took advantage of the calm and threw him off me again. We rolled around until I was on top of him this time. I pinned his hands over his head, the Wii remote having been entirely forgotten by this point. I felt his wild pulse in my hands. I looked down at him, red cheeks and open mouth, chest rising and falling. I asked myself for the first time if this was what I wanted and, if it was, could I let myself have it?

I knew he could feel me this time where our hips connected. I waited for him to react. But he didn't. He just lay there, his body tense, as if looking for the right moment to toss me off. But he didn't do that, either. For a second, I thought about it. I thought about kissing him on the mouth.

"Okay," I said, finally relenting, "can we play the Wii now?"

Life is like that, Addicted. You get your intense moments of sexual awakening, and they're bookended by the most mundane shit possible—talking your friend out of egging someone's car and then playing Wii tennis in his grandma's house. We played it like two zombies, smacking the virtual ball back and forth, hoping the physical revelation we had just mutually experienced would fade into the background. But it didn't.

"Do you wanna, like, go to sleep?" Corey asked at around nine p.m.

"Yeah," I said, thoroughly ashamed. "That sounds good." I got ready for bed in his grandma's bathroom. I looked at myself in the mirror and had one of those moments you're only supposed to have if you're the main character in a deeply depressing gay indie film, beholding my own face staring back at me and wondering, *Who am I?*

Corey was already in bed under several layers of quilts, pretending to have fallen asleep the moment his head hit the pillow. I thought it was punishment of some kind. I wrapped up my existential crisis and joined him. I felt an unbearable warmth emanating from his body, and I could hardly believe that only a few short hours ago I had touched him, and that I hadn't savored touching him. I allowed myself, finally, to fantasize—my hands running up and down his back, across the rise and fall of his muscles, hard, then soft, then kissing him, then whatever came after that. I didn't really know.

To my surprise, his foot wandered close to mine, the sole connecting with my skin. How was I supposed to live like this? I wondered. Touching, then not touching, pretending to forget, never calling it what it was for fear of losing my only friend. Foot to foot, I was alone and trapped and horny and hopeless. We would wake up the next day, and Corey would cook the eggs we hadn't used for vandalism, and life would go on. It seemed unusually cruel.

This miserable purgatory dragged on for almost a year, well into my freshman year in college. Until we took a road trip to

Austin. We wrote a list of things we'd need, picked up a pamphlet of things to do, and within days we were driving south down the highway.

By then, I knew our dynamic wasn't healthy. We'd started to fight. The topics were unimportant, but the urge to fight was overpowering. I told him he said "okay" too many times in every sentence: *Okay, dude. Okay, so, okay. Okay, man, listen to this.* In response, he told me that I got too excited for dumb things, things like introducing him to a new restaurant or showing him one of my favorite spots in Norman. "You should just let me experience things," he said. "You don't have to hype everything up."

We accused each other of being judgmental, of being a bad friend. We were frustrated with each other, and we punished each other, but we wouldn't and couldn't leave each other.

When we arrived at the Holiday Inn where we'd booked a king-sized bed, the troubles began almost immediately. "Wouldn't you prefer twin beds?" the receptionist, who became my new worst enemy in that moment, asked with concern on her face. "I just had one open up."

"Oh!" I said. "Yes, of course. Two twins, please." I said it so urgently that I was all but shouting to the world that we were two heterosexuals with nothing but heterosexual business to attend to during our stay.

"No problem!" she said pleasantly. "I've got you rebooked."

Corey and I shrugged our bags off in our room. All the inanimate objects seemed to be homophobes: the lamp, the desk, the Gideon Bible, all of them judging me as if they knew I had preferred the king bed.

"Man," Corey muttered. "I need to take a nap."

"Yeah," I said. "Me too." In our separate beds, I turned my back to him and tried not to cry. What, exactly, had I hoped would happen? Even if we had gotten that king bed, it would have just been a few games of footsy, culminating in nada.

I woke up before Corey and decided to take a shower, hoping it would clear my mind and cleanse me of the budding regret I was feeling about the whole trip. Maybe we'd leave here merely disappointed but with a definitive understanding of what we were: just friends. That clarity would sting, but at least I'd have an answer.

I walked out of the bathroom wrapped in a towel to find Corey sprawled out on his bed, completely naked and slowly stroking his erect dick.

He looked up at me, serious and inviting. He didn't rush to hide anything under the covers. I was dumbstruck, and a bit dizzy to realize this hidden fantasy brought carelessly to life. I was exhilarated; I was terrified. Something permanent and irrevocable was unfolding.

"Hey," he said, like he had been waiting on me, and it wasn't so much his naked body that got me going—I'd seen it before anyway. Nakedness is different from nudity, and here he was nude and not merely naked, intention and invitation casting the hair on his chest, his muscles, his face that I knew so well in an entirely different, alluring light.

"Hey," I said. My body moved before my mind could caution me against it. If I spoke too much, if I made one wrong move, maybe he'd realize this was wrong, shove me away and curse me out for seeing what he was inviting me to see. I let go of my towel, got on my knees beside the bed, and I touched him.

Touching him, finally, without the recoil of pretense, without having to call it anything else. I shuddered when he touched me back; I was terrified, but I wanted this so badly. His palms were hot on my skin, and although my eyes rolled back in pleasure I maintained a steady fear that his hands would stop caressing and strike me instead.

But the more I gave in to what was happening, the more a hypothetical future opened up, one in which we could touch each other without having to worry about being caught, about being walked in on or having to dance around the subject. Would this happen again, and then again? I saw a dim, blurry—but possible—future with Corey. If I could just excavate the truth of his feelings, it would be ours.

Anyway, Addicted, we jerked each other off. When we finished, we didn't look at each other. We put our clothes on, performing routine as if this happened all the time. We just had to climb back into the skins we had left puddled on the ground, and forget.

But then we went to dinner, returned, and did it again. We didn't see much of Austin at all.

For a brief moment on our drive back to Oklahoma, I thought again that maybe this would be the beginning of a new era for us. I imagined us as boyfriends. I imagined us holding hands, even, which I had never dared to do and which I considered altogether more intimate than anything we had just done. I imagined an expansive happiness that Corey and I could fill however we saw fit.

That is not what happened, Addicted.

The closer we got to Lawton, the more Corey's demeanor changed. He became stormy, curt, and quiet. We arrived at my house in the middle of the night, his headlights reflecting off the garage door. He turned to me, more serious than I'd ever seen him, and said in a voice I hadn't heard in years, the voice he'd used to talk about God, fear, and reverence for something I couldn't see, "I want you to disappear."

I met this with silence, something I'd never done with Corey before. I always had a rebuff. I always had a comeback. When we'd first met, it was sport to me—turning his words on their heads. I think he'd liked that, and I think, even back then when I was still pretending to hate him, that I'd liked that he liked it. I'd felt like I was performing a magic trick for him. In the long arc of our relationship, I'd always had words. But not this time.

I spent the next month in a deep depression. Seeing familiar things—the streets we used to drive down, the gas station where we used to get hot dogs, Grand Cherokees that weren't his—felt like a sucker punch. I couldn't believe, wouldn't accept, that such everyday items had so utterly betrayed me. My parents asked me to eat, asked me to sleep, asked me what was wrong, but all I could say was, "I think my best friend is mad at me."

I tried to throw myself into my studies at college, but all I felt was Corey's absence. I'd talk to acquaintances, but I always somehow brought the conversation back to Corey, to what had happened, telling a completely sexless, hetero version of events to which the only real response could be "That sucks." I was looking to hear "He'll come back."

Months later, he did come back. He texted me one day as if nothing had happened. Just said, "Sup." Had I a shred of dignity, I would have—should have—ignored it. But instead, I jumped at the opportunity to see him again.

We resumed where we'd left off before Austin. I went back to obsessing over his every interaction with me, staring at the Rorschach blots of our relationship, looking for romance. I don't know what he saw when he looked at us. I only know that he wanted to fool around and call it something else.

We got physical again, and again, and again. Our time apart seemed to have taught Corey how to dissociate from what we did behind closed doors, even as what we did behind closed doors became increasingly intimate.

It might sound like he was using me. Maybe he was. But it felt like a victory. Through stubbornness and sheer force of will, I had coaxed a middle ground out of life, one where I wouldn't have to ever come out of the closet but I could still be with a man. I could have both lives; the reality, of course, was that I had neither.

We would wrestle on the ground, pinning each other down, resting on each other in dangerous pauses. One night, with me on top of him, he asked me, "Have you ever put it inside a guy?" I was too afraid to answer. Later that night, feeling emboldened by his earlier question, I asked him, "Would you ever *be* with a guy?"

"I want to be normal," he said without looking at me. It was my answer to a much larger question—*Would you ever be with me?*

His response rattled around my head for days until I finally asked if we could go for a drive and talk, not telling him that it might be the last time we did so.

On the night I decided to drop the news on him, he pulled us into our familiar destination: the Walmart parking lot. He killed the engine and let out a deep sigh. Here he was, Corey, and all the baggage that came with that unfortunate, irreversible fact.

"So, what's up?" he said, his eyes fixed on the horizon. I wanted this to be like any other difficult conversation we'd had in this car. But I suspected, I knew, it wasn't.

Sometimes two otherwise-fine people end up here, with a massive tally of strikes between them. Sometimes there are so many strikes that it's no longer realistic to parse out whose is whose, to separate injury from injury. The question of blame becomes irrelevant. Blame is for simpler arrangements.

"I'm gay," I said, and just like when we touched for the first time I said it without stopping to think, knowing that thinking would hinder me. "So, there's that."

He put his hand to his chin to ponder that, and for a moment I imagined him saying "Me too" or "Same" or something like that. I imagined it all being possible, all the things I had wanted for us, even though I had come to this parking lot knowing this could kill the possibilities that had so seduced me.

I think that's the hardest part about letting someone go, Addicted. We have all these scenarios and secret hopes that we cling to. In my case, I think I knew they'd never happen. But I didn't want to find out, because finding out would remove the possibility of *what if*. I'd grown accustomed to the tyranny of optimism.

"That's cool, man," he said, like I had just told him I had decided to take up competitive mini golf. "Like, you'll do good with that, you know?"

"Do good?" I asked him. It was perhaps the one answer I hadn't accounted for, which, in life, is typically the answer you get. "At . . . being gay?"

"Yeah," he said. "Like, you even convinced me to do stuff with you." We both knew I had done no such thing. But I immediately understood the purpose of what he'd said. I'd known him too long not to. He was asking for a favor. He was saying: *Take all this on yourself, please, so I can forget.* I decided I would, not only because I still loved him but also because it was, at least and at last, a final answer.

We rode in silence toward my house and the sun began spilling pink into the dark blue sky above the empty fields. I was heartbroken; I was lighter.

I imagined all the things that could happen now. I imagined them all at once. Boys and kisses and new friends I wouldn't need to hide or explain away. I imagined a version of myself, too, without Corey. I was hungry, eager to become him. Fantasies keep us going in that way—we just have to make sure we're dreaming in the right direction.

Corey dropped me off at my house for the last time. He waved me goodbye, and I waved back. Of course a part of me wanted to suddenly reverse course, to chase him down the driveway with my arms flailing around just to see if he'd stop, just to double-check, to be absolutely sure.

Looking back, I can say I'm glad I didn't.

Sometimes, Addicted, you have to just let a person roll down to the mouth of your driveway, turn their blinker on, and go.

¡Hola Papi!

I think I lost "the one." Help?

Signed,
Loveless Loser

How to Fall in and out of Love

In the summer between my junior and senior years of college, I took an internship at the Austin Film Festival on the off chance that I would become a celebrated screenwriter one day. My job, Loveless? Reading amateur scripts submitted for the competition, along with general intern tasks: picking up people's lunches, pretending to be knowledgeable about indie films, and sending the occasional email.

I liked it fine. I wasn't particularly good at it, as I lacked basic skills in communication, organization, and memorizing coffee orders. In fact, I'm not sure why they even hired me. But I was definitely literate, and I enjoyed axing the screenplays that had zero chance of winning.

I was meant to be the first line of defense against the truly heinous typo-ridden scripts that would offend the eyes of judges higher up the ladder, which made up the lion's share of the submissions. I appreciated these bad scripts in my own way: I loved the hallmark prose of bad screenplays; the manic, unhinged writing style that read like a long Facebook rant; scripts that were seemingly written all in one go in a dark, depressing basement.

The hulking stack of unread scripts was kept in an enormous cage with a lock on it. It was intimidating to realize there were so many stories out there, all vying for the same slot. The notion that stories could fight like that, that they could arrange themselves into hierarchies, made me nervous. Because, well, how would mine stack up? I found solace in pulling out a random script, seeing a title like "THE LAST CLOWN KING OF SEXOPOLIS," reading it, and telling myself I would be fine because at least I hadn't written *that*.

I was subletting a room in a bungalow with a wooden porch and a plum door with a bronze oak-leaf knocker. My roommate was a severe PhD student named Kelsey who wore long, flowing skirts; sported a buzz cut; and was studying Azerbaijani at the University of Texas. We had another roommate, an absolutely shredded marine who appeared one day, took stock of us, promptly found a girlfriend, and was never seen again, though he continued to pay rent.

Kelsey had been to all sorts of places—Iran, Mongolia, Armenia, and many other nations she was uniformly bored with. She'd tell me about the various human rights violations she'd lived under, always prefaced with a detached "yeah." "Yeah," she'd say, "you can't drive there if you're a woman." "Yeah, they had that genocide." The one place that excited her was Philadelphia. "Philly!" she'd say, eyes lit up. "God, you gotta go."

I liked the miniature life Kelsey and I fell into that summer. We took turns cooking and hosted picnics in the backyard for her

PhD friends, mostly Muslim women who smoked cigarettes and spoke cavalierly about their friends who'd been "disappeared" at airports.

Most notably, we supported each other's ill-fated romantic endeavors, dutifully signaling excitement whenever a new man came into the picture and then disparaging him for his obvious flaws when he made his exit. I went on a couple of dates with a pastry chef who sent me home with tarts once, which Kelsey said she loved at the time. When he later told me we should just be friends, she said: "Well, his tarts tasted like feet anyway. So think about that."

We had a good thing going, as good as I could hope for in any summer. Then Thomas came knocking.

I'm not a huge believer in fate, Loveless, but I don't really have a better explanation for why I responded to Thomas's message on OkCupid. I must have been bored, or feeling whimsical, or desperately horny. His profile was sparse, his picture vague—a man with tousled brown hair sitting on the back of a Jet Ski wearing a white shirt with the buttons undone, sunglasses obscuring most of his face. "Hey there," was all he said. "Hey back," I replied.

We'd barely said anything before we exchanged numbers. We were pleased with ourselves for doing so before we'd even shared any pictures, like that was something nobody ever did. We got on the phone that same evening. I was walking around barefoot on the asphalt in front of the house just before nightfall, not totally sure why I should be nervous to talk to him. He was just a pixelated bro on a Jet Ski, for all I knew.

He had a smooth, casual voice, like he'd just woken up but

didn't mind talking. *No, go right ahead, I'm up*, his voice seemed to say. "Howdy," he said. "So, uh, how are ya?"

"You sound nervous," I said, as if I weren't.

He laughed. "Come on, man, don't make this harder on me."

"Oh, this is hard?" I said. I turned into this person with guys I liked. When good chemistry became indiscernible from gentle bullying, it meant I was on the right track. "I can let you go if you're in pain . . ."

"No, no," he said. "You stay right there."

We covered all the bases. Thomas's dad was a cattle rancher just outside Houston, and he was in his final year as a math major at the University of Texas. I was excited because I thought of myself as a person who was drawn to numbers people, people who were grounded in practical matters and held an enviable competence—the opposite of people like me, anxious creatives. I told him I was from a small town in Oklahoma. We made *Brokeback Mountain* jokes about ourselves and then we talked f. another three hours, words falling into place without effort, not much being said. But it was nice, and easy. We decided we should meet up in person as soon as humanly possible, with the stipulation that he wear his cowboy boots to complete the whole rancher fantasy.

"A cattle rancher!" Kelsey praised me like I had caught an impressive fish. She must have confused Thomas's dad for Thomas himself, or perhaps she'd conflated the two for narrative's sake. "Gah, I'm excited for you. Doesn't get more Texas than that."

"He's hot," I said. "Like, I haven't really seen him yet, but I just know, you know? It's the way he talks. He talks like a hot person."

"Well, let me know when to skedaddle on over to Brad's," she said. Brad was her latest man, a grungy musician who wore a ring on every last one of his fingers and whom Kelsey liked to speak of as if he were the world's biggest chore. "Going to Brad's show," she'd said once, rolling her eyes and slipping a leather jacket over her shoulders. She went to all his shows.

We arranged a good evening for all parties involved. Kelsey skedaddled for Thomas's six p.m. arrival. I tried to keep myself distracted, running around the block, going to the grocery store, anything to keep my mind off the growing knot in my stomach. But it was no good. I'd never felt that way before meeting a man; in the past I hadn't even noticed my feelings growing in the direction of romance. It had never been an intentional destination. This time, I was already crossing my fingers for something special, even if nothing thus far lent itself to that.

My phone buzzed, a blessing. "On my way," he said.

I paced around the hardwood floor, not sure what had come over me. It had been a good conversation, great, even, but I didn't think one promising phone call warranted this giddy, embarrassing energy. Finally, the doorbell rang—*Who rings doorbells anymore?*—and I straightened my shirt and took a deep breath.

Strangely enough, Loveless, I reversed course and hoped for disappointment in the moment I reached for the doorknob. I secretly hoped that I would open that plum door to find some guy, just some guy, regular and passable like most guys were. We could blow each other and part ways, and I could throw out the feeling that had been snaking through me all day. I could be done with it and avoid everything it was threatening me with.

But seeing Thomas on the other side of the threshold, I immediately knew he wouldn't be *some guy*. I don't believe in love at first sight or anything, but I do believe in whatever that was, a strong hunch that something important was happening.

"Howdy," he said, smiling sheepishly, sorry for being a real person after all. He was tall with wide shoulders, green eyes, and scruff on his face. He wore a green button-down shirt carefully tucked into a pair of tight, crisp jeans, and canvas sneakers on his feet.

"Nope," I said. "Try again."

"Excuse me?" he said.

I pointed at his sneakers. "Those aren't cowboy boots," I said.

"They're in my car."

"Then come back later."

"Aw, come on, man," he said, smirking.

"I'm serious," I said, and closed the door in his face.

The bell rang again and I opened the door. He did a little tap dance. "Happy now?"

The block heels of his boots made hard clunking sounds on the floor. He seemed to me to have an inappropriate weight to him, having gone from a pixelated image to a thumping presence with physical heft. I felt frightened for a moment, by his good looks, by his capacity to turn around and walk away.

"Uh," I said, "do you want anything to drink?"

We took a couple beers to my bedroom, where I revved up Netflix as a matter of formality and selected *Thor*. He took off his boots and we lay down next to each other, the laptop situated between us at the foot of the bed. I wondered, for a moment, if we would just watch the movie in relative silence at this awkward distance. That would have destroyed me. But his hand wandered close to mine. He stroked it with his fingers, so gently and earnestly it took me by surprise. I slid my hand into his, wriggled closer to him, and put my head on his chest. His heart was racing. "You're still nervous?" I asked.

"I'm passionate," he said, correcting me.

I kissed him. It was the kind of kiss that makes teenagers stupid, the kind I'd missed out on during my years in the closet. I understood what it meant to melt. I privately vowed to revisit mushy songs and books, wielding this new understanding, to enjoy them as they were supposed to be enjoyed now that I knew, now that I got it. *So this is it,* I thought, over and over, kissing and kissing. *This must be it.*

Thor ended at some point while we were tangled up in each other. We'd pause here and there to appreciate the sensation moving through us, like a natural phenomenon to look at and take in. I was used to perilous pauses in intimacy—I was so used to wondering what would happen next, if men would push me away or disappear altogether. But here I felt a safety so absolute that there was no second-guessing.

Evening turned to night without my noticing. "So," I said, several beers in, my lips raw, "what do you want to do?"

"I'm doing it," he said.

"But what do you want to *do*?" I asked, starting to get up.

"I told you," he said, pulling me back down. I buried my head in his chest, sickly sweet, but inside I was starting to panic. This was a new kind of intimacy. I'd been kissed before and touched before, but not in any way that was telling a story worth repeating, nothing beyond pleasure or pretend.

"Want another beer?" he asked, getting up.

"Oh, so *you* get to leave the bed," I said.

"Damn, I'm here trying to serve you beer and getting nothing but attitude," he said. "You're welcome." Naked, he slid his boots back on, as a kind of joke. "Be right back, Your Highness. Don't go nowhere."

"I hate beer!" I called after him, to no response. I watched him go, the blue light from the window casting delicious shadows on his back. For a moment in this silence I felt I had everything I could possibly want, and that in the next moment it could be gone. The thought of having to go back to dating apps, back to the wilderness of desire, of disappointing dates and hookups that never went anywhere beyond that, was gutting.

Before I'd known what it could look like for me, before I'd dared put a man's face on it, I'd known that I wanted to be in love. I wanted to share things I hadn't shared. I wanted to see the world as one can only see it when in love, the way love makes possibilities out of everything. I wanted to see myself through the eyes of someone who loved me, to see the facts of my everyday existence turned supernatural.

I began to feel this, already, after only one night together. I had the good sense to know I was being naïve, but naïveté was an important ingredient, I reasoned. That's what dumb love was. I wanted my turn to be reckless.

We spent the night together. Lying in bed, we took turns playing our favorite songs on YouTube, filling out the map of

interests and stray life events worth mentioning. "Is this weird?"
I asked him.

"What do you mean?" he said.

"I don't know," I said. "It doesn't usually go like this for me."

He paused, mulling that over. "I don't really know how it's supposed to go." It turned out that Thomas wasn't out to his friends
and family; he had only recently come out to himself.

"But you like guys?" I asked.

He punched me on the shoulder. "Want to take a guess?"

"Well, you can know but not *know*, you know?" I said.

"What?"

"It's like . . . I've met people who know . . . but don't *know*."

"Well, I know."

"Okay, cool." I stared at the ceiling fan. "So am I your first, or
whatever?"

"Yeah," he said. "Is that bad?"

"No, no," I said. "Not at all."

But it was kind of bad. I was more certain than ever that when
Thomas left my house in the morning it would be the last time
I ever saw him. He would kiss me goodbye, feeling pretty good
about the whole thing, and then he would climb into his car and
marinate in lethal silence. He would have to sit with what he'd just
done, and it would scare him, and I wouldn't hear from him again
for another six months, when I'd wake up to a drunken "hey" text
at three in the morning.

We were trying to sleep. I pulled him even tighter to me, and
he responded with an assuring squeeze. *Remember this*, I told
myself, running my hand over the small of his back, clinging to his

warmth to savor later, wishing that I could make this a checkpoint like in a video game and all I'd have to do to come back to it was die and die and die. *Remember what this feels like.*

The next morning went roughly as I expected. We got up. We kissed each other through the grogginess. I told him I had to get to work (calling my internship "work" was a fun bit), and he got dressed. It was an exciting, scary moment to witness, his buttoning up the shirt he'd shown up in, climbing back into the person he'd been at the door before we'd really met. I worried that I'd failed to seduce that person, the one standing in front of me wearing the shirt, and I'd spent the night with someone else. "I'll see you later?" he asked.

"Duh," I said.

Then I drove to the office, all but mourning Thomas, who had already fallen off the face of the earth, I was certain. At work, I paced the room. I tidied up the script cage for the umpteenth time. But the anxiety didn't go away. I alphabetized the screenplays and sorted them into their genres to distract myself, but the scripts only made me feel worse.

So many people had big plans for their lives, Loveless. These people, all these people and their screenplays—every one of them probably imagined winning. Even if they'd misspelled every other word and had neglected to format anything correctly, they all shared that private, intoxicating vision of getting what they'd longed for. But almost none of them would, and almost all of them had been doomed from the start without even knowing it. They wouldn't know it until they were told so.

I decided I wanted to know.

I pulled out my phone. "Hey," I started. "I had an amazing time with you." But wasn't that desperate and corny? I tried again. "Had a great time," I wrote, playing it cooler. But I found I couldn't send it.

What was so wrong with telling the truth, Loveless? What was so wrong with putting everything out there? I ran the risk of chasing him away, I supposed. But then: so what? "Hey," I wrote. "I really like you. I haven't felt this way about someone so quickly before. I don't know how you feel, but I just wanted to tell you that I want to see you again." Before I could stop myself, I hit send.

My bravery fell away like a shelf of snow from a roof, revealing absolute cowardice. *Shit*, I thought. *Shit*. I was poisoning my blessings, pushing too hard. I put my phone on silent and turned the vibration off, vowing not to face it again until that night, when his response or lack thereof would tell me everything. Fighting every impulse I had to check my messages, I threw my phone in the glove compartment of my car and drove to the grocery store on my way home.

I walked through the aisles like a zombie, eyes on the ground, feeling like I might vomit going over the contours of our time together and trying to divine his likely answer from the most insignificant details.

"Well, look who it is." A man's voice came from behind.

It was Dave.

Dave was one of the aforementioned ill-fated endeavors I'd indulged in earlier in the summer. We had found each other on Grindr. He was a city planner with a chic apartment furnished with those expensive lamps that come in weird, luxurious shapes.

Dave had silver streaks in his black hair and steely gray eyes, which were beautiful but impossible to describe without cringing, as I'd discovered when I'd told Kelsey about them. "My God," she'd said. "Please don't ever say 'steely' again. Say it any other way."

"I guess they looked kind of like a husky dog's?"

"Yes, say that."

Dave was so attractive that I'd decided to try bottoming for the first time simply because he'd asked me to. He'd seemed experienced, being in his midthirties and such, and I supposed I wouldn't mind my first time being in a nice apartment with fancy sheets. I warned him I was fresh out of the closet and hardly knew what was what, but he assured me he would be careful. He made us Negronis, which I hated with my life but sipped casually as if I were an entirely cultured person who'd seen everything there was to see.

"Shall we?" he asked, shepherding me along with a sultry smile to his bed, and I wondered how long I had been depriving myself of these real-life erotic-novel scenes because I'd been too afraid to unclench my hole.

Taking my clothes off, I must have looked like I was preparing to be executed, because he asked, "Are you sure you want to do this?"

"Yes," I said with my eyes shut. "Why?"

He got on top of me, and I think he enjoyed himself, but I found the whole process a bit clinical, with Dave occasionally whispering in a low voice, "You're doing great," like I was giving birth. When we finished, he took me out to Kerbey Lane, an all-day-breakfast café with specialty pancakes like carrot cake and lemon poppy seed.

"Here's that lemon glaze," the waiter, a young, probably gay guy with his hair in a bun, said, sliding over an aluminum cup. "It looks kind of dirty, doesn't it?" He meant it looked like cum.

"Does it?" I asked innocently.

"I think we're good here," Dave told him sharply.

"Gotcha," the waiter said. "I'll check back on y'all soon."

"Unbelievable," Dave said when the waiter was gone.

"What?"

"He was flirting with you right in front of me," he said.

"Wait, really?" I asked. No one had ever really flirted with me in public before. Either that, or I'd been too stupid to notice and never had someone like Dave around to point it out. I'd never felt so desired, like the most beautiful lobster in the tank, waiting to be eaten. "Is this what being a bottom is like all the time?" I asked.

"So young," Dave said with a wink. "You enjoy it, okay?"

Anyway, Loveless, that was Dave.

"What are you doing here?" I asked him in the frozen vegetable aisle of the grocery store.

"Some of us have to eat," he said. "Sad, but true. What about you?"

"Oh, yeah," I said. "I'm just walking around, I guess."

He asked me if I wanted to join him for a night swim at Barton Springs, a public outdoor swimming area in Austin that was free after a certain hour. "A night swim," he called it, which made the water sound like an altogether more alluring affair. I said yes and left my car in the parking lot.

"Are you okay?" he asked on the ride over. "You're quiet."

"I want to die," I explained. "I told this guy how I feel today." It didn't strike me as odd to open up about a current romantic pursuit with an old one, perhaps because of the solipsism of being twenty-one, or perhaps because of how Dave seemed to regard me, how utterly nonthreatening I was and how amusing and fake my dilemmas seemed to be to him.

"Oh, and how do you feel?"

"Strongly."

"And what did he say?"

"I haven't checked yet," I said. "Ah, shit. I left my phone in my car."

"We can go back and get it."

"That's okay," I said. "It might be for the best."

"You shouldn't avoid things like that," he said. "It's always better to just bite the bullet. Always."

"Yeah," I said, absently staring out the window and measuring the pros and cons of opening the door and rolling out.

The cold, black water at Barton Springs shocked me back into my body. Dave's black hair was slicked down over his forehead, making him look every bit the leading man in a movie, and I entertained the notion that I was going to be all right with or without Thomas. There were other guys, other bodies, and other memories to make at night. But then again, to what end?

Maybe I would just go home with Dave and get more pancakes out of it.

"You should really go look at your phone," Dave said while we dried off. "Just rip the Band-Aid off. It's always the best policy. Always."

"Why do you always say 'always'?"

"I only say it when I'm right."

"Which is . . . ?"

"Always."

"Yes, thank you, I saw that coming."

"Well done."

We sat in silence for a while. I listened intently to the crickets, hundreds of thousands of millions of crickets making noises at night for no good reason.

"So how long have you known this guy?" Dave asked.

"A few hours," I said.

"Ah."

More crickets.

"Rip the Band-Aid off," he said again.

"I could bleed to death," I said.

"Someone's being dramatic," he said. "Just give it a few years." Dave was always threatening me with getting older, like some horrible Lovecraftian wisdom was waiting for me just around the corner.

He dropped me off in the parking lot next to my car. The jolt of his aquatic beauty in the pool had faded, and I found myself wanting to go home and bury myself in a pillow. We said goodbye, and I promised to keep him abreast of my ridiculous little life and the accompanying foolish antics.

I slid inside my car, opened the glove compartment, and took a deep breath. I tapped the home button to reveal complete blackness—my phone had died.

"Are you fucking kidding me?" I asked aloud. And then it seized

me: a flight of fancy, an inkling that quickly became certainty—
the moment I turned that phone on, I would have my answer. I
would know, and then it would be over with.

I started the car and drove home as fast as I could get away
with. I pulled up to the curb, threw the car door open, and hopped
out, prepared to all but sprint to the front door, when I noticed a
figure standing on the porch next to the plum door.

"Well, shit," Thomas said. "Here you are."

Thomas, as it turned out, felt the same way I did, something
I could have found out roughly ten minutes after I'd told him
so over text earlier that day. Feeling like I was lucid dreaming, I
walked with Thomas into the house and to my room, where we fell
into each other. "I've been talking about you," he told me, beer on
his breath. "I talked about you with my friends today." He seemed
proud.

"Oh yeah?" I said.

"Yeah," he said. "I get it now."

"You get what?"

"Why guys talk about the girls they date," he said. "My friends
can't shut up about the girls they're dating. I used to get annoyed.
But now I get it. You're not a girl, but yeah. Ugh. You know what I
mean. I just like telling people about you. I really—" I kissed him.

For a solid week, there was nothing but Thomas. We made out,
had sex, went grocery shopping, ate, drank, and repeated. When I
think of love, what it feels like to be in love, I still think of the grocery store in Austin—Thomas waiting in line holding four plastic
containers of sushi for us to eat later. I'd go to grab more beer and
return from where he couldn't see me, watching him exist for a

moment, how he must have existed all the time, a stranger walking around with private thoughts and feelings and concerns. Only, he wasn't a stranger anymore, because he'd let me inside. I knew secrets about this person; we shared secret feelings. Our collusion was thrilling. To realize happiness wasn't just a possibility, but the natural thing to do, was revolutionary. How could it not be?

But of course, eventually I'd have to go back to Oklahoma.

Thomas stayed over for my last night in Austin, and we said goodbye in the doorway the next morning. "You'll call me on the way home?" he asked. "Of course," I said. It was a dramatic farewell, Loveless, our standing there, refusing to let each other go a few steps away from the plum door, where this whole thing had started. I didn't know what would happen when we walked out of it together.

I have found that things beginning with a bang don't usually end with one. Most of the time they sort of spread out and cool off as a matter of entropy, as part of the grand cosmic plan all things have to eventually become still. Thomas called me twice on the way home. Then he called me once the next week, when I was back at my parents' house and waiting for school to start. He texted me a couple times the week after that, and then he started ignoring the things I sent him. When he finally responded once in October, he told me simply, "I'm talking to someone else."

I was devastated. I was certain, Loveless, that I'd lost the one. I thought there was a Thomas-shaped cavity in my soul that would never be filled again. I thought about him most nights. I played with texting him or calling him, failing to believe the time we'd spent together was over and there was no going back to it. When I got drunk with friends, I'd talk about him. When I had free time, I'd try to write about him, but I found everything I wrote too baroque, too saccharine, too melodramatic, and I'd give up, wondering how I was supposed to capture the scope of my feelings and the great tragedy of my loss without resorting to desperate clichés.

It was almost a year later that I would return to Austin. My college roommate wanted to go, and who was I to turn down another ill-fated road trip to Texas? We drove down together and stayed in a motel. On the ride over, I texted Thomas, as I knew I would, telling him I was visiting and that I'd love to see him, and to my surprise he texted back. He said he'd be down to get lunch. I dressed up in our shitty motel room and headed to a bar where we'd agreed to meet.

I privately hoped, Loveless, that things would reignite. I told myself we were still the same elements we'd been before. The same chemical reaction was entirely possible—logical, even. We would see each other, and we would remember why our time together had been so special, and maybe he'd invite me over to his house and I wouldn't have to sleep on the air mattress on the floor in the Motel 6 (my roommate was incredibly cheap, so we'd booked a single bed and took shifts on the ground).

The bar had a tacky seventies theme and a plain menu of burgers, fries, and grilled chicken. I got there first. I slid into a booth and pretended to be enraptured by the menu while I waited for Thomas to arrive, my heart thumping as it had a year before.

A man walked in. Thomas, but not Thomas. He was limping. He lumbered up and slid into his seat opposite me. "How's it goin'?" he said, his voice familiar but coarser. He had white whiskers poking out of his beard and bloodshot eyes. He sounded lazy and uninterested, as if there were any number of things he could have been doing right then, but here he was as a matter of obligation.

"Good to see you," I said, ashamed of my own eagerness in the face of his apathy. "Are you all right? You're limping."

"Yeah," he said. "Got into a fight." He said it so simply, as if it were something I should have guessed.

"Did you win?" I asked.

"No," he said.

He told me things hadn't really worked out with the other guy he'd been seeing, but that was fine, because he wasn't really interested in seeing anyone, he said. He hadn't told anyone else he was gay since we'd last seen each other. He didn't feel he needed to. He said all these things with a callous boredom, pointed, I thought, at my silly idea of meeting up again. "I see," I repeated, reduced to an idiot who only said one thing. "I see."

"Well," he said, food still on his plate, "I better get going soon."

"Yeah," I said, wondering who this person was. "Same here." It was a feeble attempt at saving face, at pretending I hadn't wanted anything in particular. I got up and, feeling drunk but sober, wobbled along in front of him to the exit.

A terrible possibility was unfolding in front of me. "Well, it was nice to see you," he said, somewhat kinder than before, perhaps apologizing in a small way for not caring.

"Yup," I said, seizing on what little high ground he'd afforded me. I walked the other way, pretending that was where I'd parked, and left him. After I'd made some distance on the sidewalk, I saw him limping off in final mockery of everything I'd held on to so childishly over the past year. I ducked into an antiques store, unwilling to face the world after such an utter humiliation, and sequestered in a corner under a heap of knickknacks, I cried into my hands.

The terrible possibility was that maybe the Thomas I'd been so enamored with hadn't really gone away. It could very well have been that he'd never existed in the first place. This Thomas, the haggard one with bloodshot eyes and no warmth to spare, had been the same Thomas from that summer. Maybe love, or its evil sibling, infatuation, had made him something else in my eyes. When I thought about it, really thought about it, what had been his defining features? What had his personality really been? Who had he been other than a man who had excited me?

And what if it wasn't Thomas I had been missing all this time? What if it had been the act of loving—the moving through life while loving, the way of seeing myself while loving, the splendid shapes love makes of the world, the way it takes the mundane and twists it into something altogether worthier?

He was probably in his car now, driving back to some house I'd never seen, to a life I actually knew next to nothing about, and never would, and all the things he knew about me—my favorite songs, the parts of my body I didn't like that were more sensitive or ticklish, the stories about my family and about Oklahoma, things that had once added up to something special, potent trappings of an interesting person worth getting to know—were now reduced to trivia. I hardly cared about them myself, in that light.

I took a night drive through Austin, indulging in the exquisite, gentle pangs of nostalgia. There was Barton Springs. There was the grocery store. Where was Dave? And there was the house, the plum-colored door with the oak-leaf knocker, the only thing that had remained more or less the same, a faithful friend.

I drove by the film festival office and its cage full of scripts. I had a notion then, one that made me feel a little better and one that has stuck with me over the years, a new way to look at memory.

What if, Loveless, memory is an act of creation? Our brains don't hold perfect records of the things that have happened, a Rolodex we can cycle through and call upon for official accounts. Maybe remembering is the same thing as imagining. Maybe I had imagined Thomas, imagined a man who loved me so that I could love myself, imagined a story wherein a handsome stranger had fallen into my lap one summer and made life worthier of living.

But then, no. Not quite. Not perfectly quite. There had been something real about Thomas, about the whole thing. It hadn't been exactly as I remembered, but that didn't negate everything I felt, everything I knew to be true. My question, then, now that it was good and over, was: could it be enough?

Was it enough to have experienced what I had, knowing I would never have that same experience precisely again? Could I live with knowing that it had been part fact and part fiction, and that disentangling one from the other would be impossible?

Yes, I think so. I think it is enough. Love is nothing without fiction. It's a story, and like any story it can be told well or told poorly. And, Loveless, I think the idea of "the one" is the wrong way to write your story about love. "The one" is convenient. It lets us organize the mess of our past romantic endeavors into a binary of failure—there were the ones who revealed themselves as failures, that didn't work out, but they were in the service of helping us find "the one," the one whom we've been searching or waiting for.

I'm not sure that person exists at all. I think there are simply important people in our lives. They don't always stay important. They don't always stick around. But the point at which we meet them, the point on the grid where our lives intersect, is a sacred thing. It makes them "the one" in that moment; just because that moment ends, it doesn't mean it's any less special. You can't help but romanticize it, make stories out of it, think about it when it's gone, as long as you don't linger there.

I was in love once. I was happy to be in love. I was sad for a while when I wasn't. I'm glad it happened, and that it's over. I do hope it happens again.

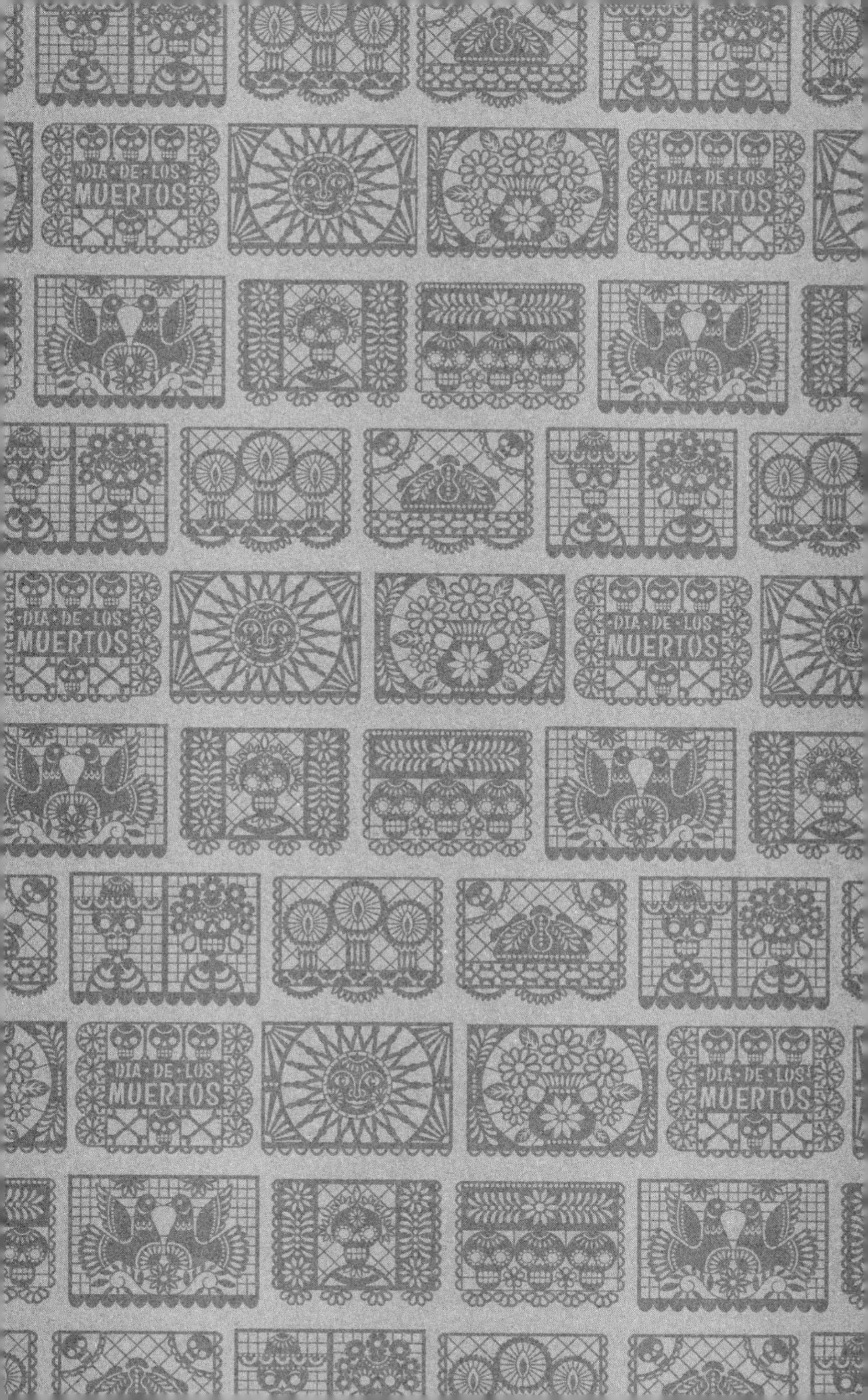

¡Hola Papi!

How do I forgive and forget?

Signed,
Unapologetic

How to Chat with Your Childhood Bully over a Gay Dating App

My hometown provides slim pickings in terms of hookups, Unapologetic. As a generally lecherous person who enjoys casual sex, this is bad news for me, as it means I must simply go without whenever I visit home, like I'm some kind of ascetic monk. That doesn't mean I don't try. Oh, I try. I will open up Grindr, or Scruff, or Tinder, and desperately troll for some dirty, sexy chat. I've spent a lot of my time on the international "explore" feature of Scruff, chatting up bearded dudes from Brazil in broken Portuguese. Maybe I wouldn't have to do this if there were anything else to do in Cache, but there isn't really, unless you're into vaping or looking at prairie dogs.

"The grid," the nearby profiles, has stayed pretty much the same in my hometown for all of my visits. The nearest profile to my parents' house is about two miles away and reliably dons a profile picture of a human head with gazelle horns sprouting out of it, mounted on a wall. The profile's stats are listed as "white" and "six feet tall" and "just browsing."

Not really my type!

Anything closer than two miles, mind you, would be cause for alarm, as there isn't much but fields all around the house. I once saw a profile located a few hundred feet away and had to look outside and scan the horizon for someone hiding among the wheat. A glitch.

I went home for Thanksgiving one year. (At the time, I was living in DC, working as a blogger for a doomed content mill.) The leaves had changed and there was a crisp, cold nip in the air. I would go for walks, bored out of my mind in between watching the news with my abuela ("I would kill Dick Cheney myself if I could, mijo") and sexting Bulgarians on Scruff. I was on one of these walks when I got a Scruff notification of a more domestic kind: the profile was two miles away.

"Hey," it said. I was used to fielding messages from faceless profiles in my brief career as a chronic sex-haver. In bigger cities, I'd ignore these brief missives. But without much else to do in my neck of the woods, I decided to entertain it.

"What's up?" I asked. A few minutes passed.

"I think you know me," the mystery profile responded.

I immediately conjured some suspects.

First, there were my hopes: maybe it was a former football player from my high school, one of the guys who'd been a part of the Fellowship of Christian Athletes. There'd always been some sexual tension there between us. "We went to middle school together," the next notification said.

Hope turned to panic. This person had definitely gone to school with me in Cache, which was much closer to my current location. So they'd been present for the worst years of my life. "Were we friends?" I stupidly asked. I hadn't had any friends back then, but I couldn't outright ask, *You wouldn't happen to be one of the people from my night terrors, by any chance?*

"You might not like me," he said. "I was a little mean to you haha."

My middle school experience was no matter for "haha"-ing, Unapologetic. With terror bubbling up in my gut, I wondered which one he had been. I was pacing in circles around the house. "Who?" I finally gathered the courage to ask.

He sent me a picture, a husky guy standing in front of a tractor with his hands shoved into Wrangler jeans, a blank smile on his face as if he hadn't wanted to take a picture. It was Dillon.

Dillon had been the one who'd slapped me across the face with a hot dog and said, "Do you like wieners? Faggots like wieners, right?" He'd put his arm around me and walked me to and from the cafeteria many times, whispering in my ear, "Ew, do you like this?"

That was Dillon.

The way he'd used touch against me had been so specific and effective, always asking me if I liked it. He had gradually planted the thought in my head: *Isn't it wrong to like this?* That fear, that doubt, perhaps had contributed to how long I'd stayed in the closet. And yet, all that time, had Dillon been in there with me? This added another chilling layer to the way he'd touched and prodded me. It made me feel a little nauseated; I didn't know it was possible to make my memories of middle school even worse. But that's one thing about life, Unapologetic. Things can always, always get worse.

"Are you mad at me?" he asked.

I paced around the house, recalling, of all things, a tree outside my old apartment in Oklahoma City. It was warped like a big fishhook. The tree had grown up and around an object, perhaps a boulder, instead of straight up. The object, whatever it was, was later removed, resulting in the tree's strange trajectory. That was me: a weird-ass tree that had grown up, around, and in spite of Cache, in spite of Dillon, bending myself around obstacles even after they had long disappeared.

It was astounding to think that Dillon still had the audacity to hit me up on Scruff. "Do you remember what you did?" I asked.

"No lol," he wrote. "But I was a real asshole back then." I thought that was putting it rather mildly.

All those years of remembering, carrying, and suffering over this person, and he probably hadn't thought about me at all since I'd moved away. I was willing to bet all my tormentors were also suffering from this kind of amnesia—they didn't think about, care about, or remember what they'd done to me. The axe forgets; the tree remembers.

"Are you mad?" he asked again.

It was a question worth considering, Unapologetic. Indeed, was I mad? I looked again at the picture he'd sent me. I'd recognized him instantly, but of course he wasn't the kid who'd bullied me in school. He was taller, was thinning a little up top, and was for all intents and purposes an adult now. It seemed wrong that he should be an adult, that time had impacted him at all, static as he was in my head, a perpetual baby-faced nightmare.

Here was the dilemma. Maybe forgiving this adult person who

was and wasn't my former bully was possible. We'd both grown and changed. The more distance I had from my youth, the easier it was for me to see the person I'd been in middle school. I'd been antisocial—rude, even—and had coped by building a superiority complex, pretending I was hated because I was smarter and better than everyone else. Surely, I'd hurt people, too. Surely, I was big enough now to make peace with this person from my past.

On the other hand, was this not a classic line of thinking for a victim of abuse, being too magnanimous in the face of my own misery? I had a nasty habit of letting people run all over me. I'd seen it in action. At work, I'd been promised a raise two times already, and both times the promises had been broken despite my numbers being better than everyone else's; I always moved on from these disappointments without complaint. I tended to shrink myself, afraid of the consequences of causing too much of a fuss. My experiences with abuse had informed this practice, made everyone out to be a bully-in-waiting, and it behooved me to avoid bringing that out in people, lest I become my middle school self again, helpless and pathetic.

What if, Unapologetic, my urge to forgive Dillon came from that place? What if it stemmed from my desire to avoid conflict, to make things as convenient as possible for others at my own expense?

I walked, and I pondered. If rural Oklahoma is good for one thing, it's walking and pondering. I breathed into my hands to warm my nose as I crunched along the gravel road leading to my parents' house.

I put myself in Dillon's cowboy boots. What must it have been like, I wondered, to be a closeted farmer's kid in Cache? What would lead a person to do the things he'd done, other than self-hatred? I couldn't know for sure, but what I did know was that he wasn't the one-dimensional villain I'd made him out to be. All this time, and he'd been closeted, too. Yes, he had hurt me; yes, he, too, was a victim. We'd grown up in the same town, where being gay was among the worst things one could be. When he'd been pushing me around, he must have just been relieved it wasn't him. I might not have been able to forgive that, but I could at least understand it. I might have even done the same thing.

I think violence is a circle, Unapologetic. A circle that uses violence to perpetuate itself, leaving in its wake people who are both victims and villains in turn. Someone had made Dillon hate himself. He saw himself in me. And so, he hated me. Life was not a matter of perfect villains getting in my way. I was not immune from the internalized hate that had galvanized Dillon to do what he'd done to me. I, too, even if in my own quiet way, had been someone's villain.

In public spaces, when I heard a gay man speaking in a flamboyant, feminine way, sometimes I would reflexively cringe, wishing he'd tone it down. There had been times I'd seen people dress in gender-nonconforming ways and felt secondhand embarrassment or shame for them. I wasn't just policing others, either. I hated my own voice. I'd tell myself my taste in clothes was too feminine, that I could *never* go out wearing *that*. I'd never be successful enough, good enough, until I had the right kind of body, the right kind of attitude, was the right kind of man. Examining this was a bitter pill to swallow.

I had to ask myself if it was possible to fully break the cycle. Was it even possible to undo all the programming, to triumph over the critical voice in my head? I suspected it would be impossible to ever truly, completely unlearn the things I'd been conditioned to accept.

And yet, Unapologetic, I also considered that perhaps I wasn't in search of a destination; if violence is a circle, perhaps forgiveness is a process as well. In unlearning my tendency to be critical of myself and others, in meeting people I'd previously discounted, in marshaling my courage to express myself in ways I hadn't allowed myself to before, I'd accessed the most nourishing experiences of my life. It might make me less hateful and more accepting of the people around me; I would no longer have to examine their flaws for fear of recognizing those same flaws in me. They weren't flaws at all. That catharsis was something I wanted for everyone. Even Dillon.

I was riding the high of this philosophic victory when I received yet another message. "Want to fool around?" he asked.

Oh God, I thought as a new wave of horrific images flooded my vision. It would take me weeks, perhaps months, to scrub the nightmare of heading to Dillon's ranch and hooking up with him. It was the splash of cold water I needed.

"No," I said. "Have a good life, man."

And you know what, Unapologetic? I meant it.

¡Hola Papi!

How do you keep chasing your dreams
even though you're most definitely a failure?

Signed,
Screw-Up

How to Describe a Dick

There was a quote my middle school art teacher once made me write down, Screw-Up. She used to begin every class with a meditation on the wise words of extremely dead artists, platitudes written in Sharpie over her rickety projector. I think it was Henri Matisse who'd said it, or someone dead like that.

"There is nothing more difficult for a truly creative painter than to paint a rose," the quote said. "Because before he can do so, he has first to forget all the roses that were ever painted."

I thought of this quote as I struggled to describe the fat penis on the laptop screen before me. I had the porn film on pause. It was from one of those fancy studios that churned out glossy clips with bright lights and seamless transitions. One of the actors was about to put it in the other guy, which was as good an opportunity as any for me to describe the equipment. It looked remarkably like every penis I'd ever seen in my life, an absolute factory mold of a dick. I stared at it blankly. It stared back.

I traced the contours of its veins with my mind's eye, rifled through the descriptors I'd already used in my previous blog posts—"girthy," "fat," "rock hard." Why hadn't I saved any of those for this post? How like me to burn through everything too quickly without any consideration for the future.

Let me explain, Screw-Up. It was my first month of living and freelancing in New York City. I'd moved up from DC to write for the reboot of the "progressive blog" I used to work for. My new boss was a loose cannon who, at one point in time, held our team on the phone for an hour to read aloud a chapter of Cormac McCarthy's *The Road*, only to ask us at the end why we couldn't write blog posts about Hillary Clinton like that.

I never thought I'd miss my old job. I'd moved to our nation's capital from Oklahoma in 2013 to work at the media startup, where, within a year or so, I became the most senior staffer at the age of twenty-four after the CEO and the managing editor and all my coworkers had been let go at some time or other. When the "reboot people," as I called them, came in to check us out, they had to parley with me because everyone else had gone. My traffic numbers were good!

The reboot people were part of a larger media company with headquarters in New York City. They absorbed the startup, which at that point was just me and my friend Daphne. She made memes featuring sassy quips and inspirational quotes from various Democratic politicians. We hated our jobs.

The new boss sought me out because he'd read one post I'd done that he'd liked. It was an investigation into whether or not drinking from the red holiday Starbucks cups could, in fact, turn you gay. My results were inconclusive as homosexuality was a preexisting condition for me. He was so impressed he asked me if I'd be willing to move up to the Big Apple.

I said goodbye to my dearest friends and moved up to New York City, where I was promptly fired two weeks later for "not being passionate enough." I was summoned into an office in our swanky Manhattan workspace to meet with my boss, who I knew was about to give me the axe. I forced myself to cry. "I moved my life up here," I wailed between sobs. "My whole *life!*" Move over, Meryl Streep.

This performance seemed to do the trick, as I was offered a luxurious three months' severance. Or maybe that would have happened anyway and it was a waste of my time like everything else in the world was. Nevertheless, I found myself a writer in Brooklyn with no job, only a few bylines to my name, and precious little time to get my feet under me. I hadn't even unpacked all the boxes in my new apartment yet.

It was in this vulnerable period that I met Alex, a gay man with a baby face who found me over Facebook and, after learning I was a writer, offered me a job recapping gay porn for a small family of cheap-looking blogs with neon logos and ads for fiber supplements all over the place.

Alex lived in Prague and sent me assignments over Skype. On this particular day, the day the dick broke me, he'd given me a deadline of nine p.m. EST to finish off a batch of three recaps. I'd spent my entire morning drinking coffee and watching videos of impossibly chiseled white dudes smashing each other to smithereens.

While watching, I was to keep an eye out for GIFable

moments to include in the blog post. These moments typically revealed themselves when the camera zoomed in on a guy's face to show it contorted with pleasure, his forbidden bits hidden away so that the post itself didn't become porn rather than a winking advertisement for porn. This mattered a great deal. Ideally, the GIF would convey the sheer force of the thrusting without showing any nudity.

These moments would surface, and like a fisher with a tug on his line, I would hit pause to capture them before they could escape. I'd write some prose—"After sucking him long and deep, Cody Steele flips Lukas McMuscles over for some ass play." My Pulitzer was undoubtedly in the mail.

But after a burst of productivity, I felt the crushing weight of writer's block. Worse than that, I was having an out-of-body experience at my desk after staring at that dick for so long. A few minutes of space cadetting, and the dick stopped looking like a dick. It became a mere body part, fleshy and primitive. The word "genitals" came to mind. What an unsexy word. But sex is incredibly unsexy if you think about it, Screw-Up.

In the Google doc, I made another pass. "Cody Steele pounds his little bitch bottom with . . ." I paused; no one would get an erection from this. I would be laughed out of the smut circuit and exposed as a wannabe, as a writer who had turned to erotica after failing to hack it in journalism because he thought it would be easier. "He can't write anything, I guess," people would definitely say.

The panic attack set in. I had gone to school for professional writing. I had dreams of becoming a published (and at least moderately celebrated) author. But there I was—newly fired two weeks after moving to New York, struggling to conjure a couple of measly paragraphs about penetration so I could make rent. What a phony.

"Are you still watching porn?" my roommate asked serenely from the kitchen. It was a lovely afternoon in Brooklyn. Soft light filtered in through my curtains, and I could hear the gentle swoosh of the M train gliding to a stop outside.

Maybe it was Monday. Maybe it was Tuesday. The days of the week had stopped mattering so much since I'd gone freelance. Time was partitioned into days when I received emails (weekdays) and days when I did not (weekends). I had never hated weekends so much in my life. No one followed up on any jobs or asked me to write anything on the weekends, and I needed money. I needed money badly.

"Yes," I said. "Hey, what are some words you would use to describe a dick?"

"Want a mimosa?" he called back, either not hearing my request or ignoring it, for which I was grateful. He swished into my room holding two bulbous glasses of fizzy orange juice. "Cheers!" he said, clinking the glasses himself, then handing me one.

There were no rules back then in the lean year that I moved from DC to New York. Mimosas had escaped the boozy confines of Sunday brunch and infiltrated random slots of the weekday.

Some days, I woke up at noon. On others, I woke up at three in the morning to finish a column for the *Guardian* about whatever Trump had done on the campaign trail and why I, as a gay Mexican, vehemently condemned it. In my personal life as well as in America, nothing made sense anymore. The apocalypse was everywhere.

None of this had really been covered in journalism school, where I had been taught how to put formal pitches together for magazines and how to seal and mail them in a manila envelope. I was in a "Now what?" period of life, and I realized it with the sinking feeling of a middle school kid who'd forgotten to do his homework.

A pervasive narrative about millennials—one millennials themselves like to propagate—is that we were teed up for failure because we were told too often that we were special. We were placed in "special" programs with names like Talented and Gifted (TAG) or Advanced Placement (AP) that were held in "special" rooms and carried "special" perks, and along the way we were deluded into believing that we must really be something to write home about.

Then the reality of late capitalism stepped in, be it in the form of student loans or a bleak job market, and our lack of fortune was compounded by a profound twist of the knife: But I'm *special*. This wasn't supposed to happen to *me*.

I think there can be something to that idea while still believing it's for people whose schools had SMART Boards and, I don't know, textbooks. Lawton High had disabused me of any illusions that life was fair. The stabbings and metal detectors and "general paper shortage" taught me that life was a lottery. Being in AP classes in Lawton High just meant you had more money than other people, which was true in my case.

But I did have an inkling—chalk it up to regular old hubris— that I was "better" in some way. Not better than other people, but better than what I was being given. The notion that so many in my generation think this way because we were coddled or given too many participation trophies seems off. I think it's more about the idea of indignity. Or more specifically, the idea that our inherent dignity has been denied, molested: We want to do worthwhile work, work that satisfies us or at the very least adequately compensates us. We want to feel present in our labor. We want our labor to mean something.

These are not outlandish requests, but we make them in an environment that can't fulfill them, one where we are estranged from every tangible element of our work: our coworkers; the actual dollar value of our time; the people who make the decisions that govern our lives; the table those people are sitting at, wherever it is. In place of these concretes are intangibles: mission statements, values, and aesthetics. Open office plans and beanbag chairs also usually feature in the picture.

Industry understands this desire and uses it to its advantage, luring young people into content mills and chic startups with promises of creating not *just* a product but a *culture*, or giving space to tell *important* and *overlooked* stories. There is something violating about doing work for people you can't see, people who expect you to be a genuine believer in things they don't even believe themselves—that you're going to change the world by selling a trendy piece of luggage, that you're going to build a loving community by launching a website that caters to runners, that you're going to "uplift minority voices" by writing a blog.

These are things you, the worker, the believer, must have at your core, must carry with you into the office every morning, must strive to embody in every professional interaction you have while employed there, all so some guy who forgot he owned your company in the first place can decide to fire all of you while sitting on the toilet one day because it isn't raking him in enough money or prestige or whatever it was he felt he wanted when he threw his fortune at it.

I haven't met a single person who's ever genuinely bought into the "we're different because we care" corporate ethos that permeates our culture, Screw-Up. That gulf, the one between what we're expected to believe and what we know, creates apathy, resentment, and anxiety. Someone who grew up in a world where they didn't have to contemplate selling their plasma to make the next payment to Sallie Mae might possibly construe this cocktail of emotions as "entitlement."

But that afternoon, when I was struggling to describe the dick, I would have settled for the beanbag chair. Freelancing at home was breaking my brain. I missed having healthcare. I missed being able to wake up on weekends and know it was the weekend, and that if I didn't accomplish much today I would still be fine because I had a job. I missed, like, I don't know, fancy snacks.

I sipped my midday mimosa and refocused on the penis before me. *Oh God*, I thought. *My abuela picked fruit in this country for me to become this.*

Then there was the other side of the coin: Sure, I was disenchanted with the late-capitalist hellscape I'd been plunged into. But within its confines, in the hamster cage, I did have my heroes of industry, people I'd have liked to emulate.

In my short New York City–resident tenure, I'd already been exposed to a merciless barrage of talented writers whom I'd formerly only known as bylines or as media personalities. There were writers who'd published slim volumes of poetry that had earned them critical acclaim and won them the right to stare past me while shaking my hand, the vacant look in their eye only adding to their mystique, at least in my mind, where I conjured visions of the drugs they used and of their profound troubles.

There were writers with multiple novels under their belts who carried themselves with an enviable, disheveled bravado. To be so busy, so overworked, so entirely concerned with deadlines—I could only wish that were me. They spoke dismissively of signings and editors and "lit." Lit! Literature, the world I thought so sacred and unapproachable, they had shortened to "lit." Such was their power.

There were writers with massive social media followings who frequented happy hours where elbow would rub with elbow and spawn thousands of "likes" online. I could only imagine how it must've felt to walk with such a consensus following me around, to know that my thoughts were valid and good, because so said the internet.

I religiously compared myself to these shiny people and sought out the urgent shortcomings in myself that they helped reveal. I hadn't gone to an Ivy League school, for one, but there was nothing I could do about that. I thought my writing was good, but probably not good enough, or else it would have punched me through to better dinner parties. I cared about success, whereas they seemed so familiar with it that they'd stopped caring so much about it.

I wondered how there were so many people precisely my age and in my desired industry doing exactly what I wanted to do, and I wondered if they knew they had what I wanted right in their hands, or if that cool, jaded glaze in their eyes kept them from knowing. I envied that, too.

New York was a wilderness of mirrors—in every person I met, I saw some horrifying reflection of myself, and when they spoke, they told me all the specific ways I wasn't good enough. I wondered if this was what my life would be: harsh realities and intangible fantasies.

I considered what I could get out of the path I was on, if luck was with me. I imagined porn writing, the highs and lows of it. It really didn't *feel* all that distinct from other kinds of writing, and in many ways it was more honest. My other writing, the op-eds with their righteous, identity-based outrage, often hinged on the spectacle of trauma, a facsimile of courage: I am angry, I am brave, and here is my pain. Getting people off was at least a nobler, more serviceable goal.

I thought maybe I could get really good at it, Screw-Up. Maybe I could move to Miami, which in my mind was a neon, porny place to live. I would shave all my facial hair except for my mustache, which would grow thick. I would be invited to poolside parties with those flamingo inflatables with which every gay man with abs was always taking pictures. I would wear silky floral shirts with all the buttons undone. I would have bitches, Screw-Up—dudes I met from the porn circuit or whatever. I could write other things on the side: novels, perhaps inspired by the vapid, wrecked world I was immersed in. I would find beauty in it and I'd be inspired and preoccupied and, ultimately, okay.

But, probably, there'd just be me, staring at dicks and making GIFs forever.

I'd compromise myself into some ordinary life that would terrify me if I were to get a sneak peek of it, something that would make me want to up and quit if I knew that was what was ahead of me. Or maybe, if I was luckier still: a fancy lamp, an exposed brick wall, a healthcare plan for a year or so, a boss in a blazer and jeans lecturing me about company values, a beanbag chair.

I finished my mimosa. Another train came whooshing down the track. "Happy Wednesday!" my roommate called out, to no one in particular. Yes, it was Wednesday after all. Wednesday! What a perfectly fine day. Wednesday was right in the middle of it, the hump itself, and I needed only to come up with one measly word to describe one measly penis and be done with my task.

"Do you want another one?" my roommate called from his bedroom. He'd been taking a nap.

"No," I said. "I'm all right. Thank you, though."

And then it hit me, the word I'd overlooked because I hadn't thought it flashy enough.

"THICK!" I screamed back from my room. My roommate groaned, as if rolling back over in his bed to fall asleep again. It was only a mildly adequate word as far as descriptions of dicks go, Screw-Up. But it would do for now.

¡Hola Papi!

I want to dress gayer, but I'm afraid.

What do I do?

Signed,
Boring Closet(ed)

How to Dress Yourself
in Silks and Linens

My mom used to take me shopping with her. We'd drive up to the mall and go to Dillard's, the nicest department store in town, or sometimes we'd even go to Wichita Falls, Texas, for more options. My mom had a discerning eye for fashion that she'd brag about. "I was poor, but I had good taste," she'd often said of her childhood. "It doesn't matter how much money you have. You can have good taste."

I'd watch her rifle through the clothing rack and make her judgments by some mysterious criteria. I'd wait for her outside the changing room, holding her purse. She'd come out, pressing the garments to her body to feel them out, checking herself in the mirror. "What do you think?" she'd ask.

I loved these trips to the mall, Boring. I loved the idea of taste, the notion that I could hold some authority over distinguishing good from bad. It was like a game, and I got hooked very early. But it was a complicated addiction knowing that I was supposed to hate these outings. On one hand, I loved judging my mom's outfits, though my opinion wasn't worth half as much as she let me believe. I loved looking at the mannequins, the elegant articulation of their hands, their statuesque confidence, the stories they told with their clothes—a trip to the beach, lunch with her shady friends while their wealthy husbands were at work, a cocktail party where she was to seduce a prince.

But this fantasy world was not meant for me, a boy. My clothes were not meant to tell such stories. All they would ever say is, *I am a boy, and here I am. I am a boy at a wedding. I am a boy at school. I am a boy, and this is my shirt, thank you.* My options were limited to the "Husky Kids" section of Walmart, where I could adorn myself in such evocative fashions as a T-shirt that said NORMAL PEOPLE SCARE ME on the front and boot-cut jeans. I was in hell, Boring. I was Tantalus, the Greek mythological figure made to stand in a pool of water beneath a fruit tree, the water always receding before he could take a sip, the fruit ever eluding his grasp. I could look at the treasures before me, but I couldn't partake. In fact, I was meant to pretend I hated the whole idea of clothing and accessorizing. That was "girl stuff."

Yet there I was, the cliché closeted gay boy harboring a secret love of fashion, hiding my mom's copies of *Vogue* under my bed. But it wasn't just the clothes that drew me in, Boring. I was attracted to the idea that there was another way to go about life, one in which I was better equipped to thrive. My present criteria expected me to play sports and not cry, so I was failing.

I liked this foreign world that troubled itself with superfluous details. It was the domain of fierce women and harried men of an alternative masculinity who wore ridiculous garments and made crises out of little things like length, fit, and accessories. I imagined it as a sort of play world where everyone was acting and dressing up. They could have called off the act at any time, surely, but they were having too much fun pretending.

Glimpses into the world of high fashion came to me through my mother's magazines and *America's Next Top Model*, which we watched religiously together on the couch and where flamboyant men were always screaming at skinny women to bend their backs more. I'd privately fantasize about Tyra Banks's coming to our tiny town to scout for new models for the junior version of her show that didn't exist. She'd see me, ugly, but so ugly that I was in possession of a unique kind of beauty—interesting to look at— and she'd cart me off to do a photo shoot. That was definitely how reality television worked.

But my reality was utterly inhospitable to my interests. Cache wasn't exactly a hotbed for sartorial innovation; once, a kid wore a Hollister shirt to school—a chocolate-brown knit shirt with the red Hollister seagull on it—and initiated the trial of the century. "Isn't that for gay dudes?" he was asked. "Isn't Hollister a gay-guy thing?" I never saw the shirt again. Another time, a kid who everyone suspected was gay dared to describe his plaid button-up shirt as "cute." He was compelled to transfer schools the next year.

Instead, I held secret space in my brain for my passions— drawing, sewing, accessorizing, visions of tall buildings with shiny tiled floors and vicious women in oversized sunglasses and fur coats. I was an imagined citizen of that secret place. I was some magazine editor's exhausted, overworked assistant, scrambling to put together an outfit for the big launch party the next day.

I don't know what happened to that world, those offices in my mind. Maybe all the years in Satan's Armpit, Oklahoma, finally wore me down. At some point, I gutted them and replaced them with things that made more sense: a subdued interest in Tarantino, a highly public appreciation for video games. In high school, I dressed like a parody of a straight Mexican kid with anger issues. I wore loose jeans and baggy shirts that reflected approximately zero of my interests: Mexican soccer teams and wrestlers and platitudes that catered to athletes, slogans like JUST DO IT or PROTECT THIS HOUSE. What house? What was this house, who lived there, and why had I been tasked with protecting it? All moot points. The point was to look like I didn't care about clothes.

That's the paradox of lazy masculinity, Boring. All clothing is selected with some degree of care, even the clothing I was wearing. I wanted to look apathetic and masculine, which required a concerted effort from my costuming department.

It wasn't until years later when I was introduced to *RuPaul's Drag Race* as a senior at the University of Oklahoma that I began to think of clothing as a vehicle for self-expression. I'd found two older gay guys to take me under their wing; *Drag Race* was part of my required viewing. Sitting on the living room floor surrounded by other gay guys in wigs, I watched with some trepidation as men transformed themselves into visions, using makeup and sewing machines. What emerged wasn't a woman, necessarily, but an aesthetic assertion of glamour, or comedy, or anything, really. My takeaway was to consider clothing as a language, a visual vocabulary with which one could speak: "I'm giving the judges 'Helen of Troy if she were a lesbian mall goth.'" That was something one could communicate, if one wanted to, with a curated selection of garments. It made me wonder if I had anything I wanted to say.

I began to take my interest in fashion more seriously. I openly delighted in shopping instead of pretending to dread it as I had in my youth. I read up on textiles, leather goods, and what constituted "quality." I stepped into dressing rooms and tried everything on, appreciating the hypothetical futures each outfit illustrated. *I would wear this on a nice date. I would wear this on a vacation to the beach.* Each one had the capacity to make me a certain kind of person, a new person, whom I could step into and move through the world as.

I was excited and content with this masquerade for a while. Then I moved to New York.

My first roommate in New York was a circuit queen who occasionally hosted queer parties. He knew I wasn't a big party person—it was hard for me to stay out past one a.m. without blinking to stay awake—but he wanted to show me what I was missing out on. "It will be cute," he promised.

The party was called Holy Mountain, or HoMo. I'd watched enough *Drag Race* to know that the occasion called for *a look*, a showstopping fashion moment. But I didn't have anything in my closet that even came close to being *a look*. I selected my most eccentric piece, which, at the time, was a black leather harness I'd purchased because I was filthy first and an aesthete second. I wore it over a mesh black shirt. My roommate stirred up some pre-workout (drinkable cocaine) to amp us up and we drank it out of plastic cups on the M train to Manhattan. When we arrived, I immediately realized I was just a straight-looking bro in a harness.

I saw some wild shit, Boring. I'd seen outfits like these on TV, like on *Drag Race*. But that was TV. Tyra was never really going to jump out of the screen and ask me to pose for a photo. But here, at HoMo, it was actually happening: capes and catsuits and acrylic nails and shoulder pads and makeup like you'd see in a fantasy movie. I'd stepped into another world, a world where the hierarchies had been turned upside down and aesthetic queerness was aspirational. Passing as heterosexual, which had once been my only goal, was considered bland in this little corner of the world. I took quick stock of myself, Boring, and realized I was dull as hell.

I admit it felt a little unfair. How was I to know that the fantasy world I'd lusted over as a kid had been real all along? If I had known, if I had only known, I would have adjusted accordingly. I would have invested in the statement jewelry and the billowy tops and the platform shoes I'd admired from a distance. This was all homework I'd neglected, because I'd been so busy pretending to be straight. Years and years denying myself the things I'd wanted, and for what? To end up as some guy who thought a pair of chinos in a "fun" color was the epitome of fashion? My God. I was downright fratty.

Who, exactly, had been stopping me? In truth, no one had ever explicitly told me not to wear the things I'd wanted to wear. My parents, overall, were accepting people. Hell, looking back, my mother had all but deliberately raised a gay son.

So who, exactly, had been holding me back from being the person I'd wanted to be, and was that person in fact myself? And did this extend beyond clothing? Was this the case with the men I liked and had dated, with the interests I held and the way I spoke? Had I been mistaking other people's desires for my own all this time? I woke up the next day in my Brooklyn apartment with a hangover and an existential crisis. *I need to get so much gayer*, I thought. I went shopping as soon as my next paycheck came in.

I hit up Topman first. It wasn't exactly the boldest direction, but in truth I had no idea where the mirages I'd seen at HoMo had sourced their duds. Was there a secret store that sold capes and mesh crop tops, and if so, where was it? Or was every gay person in New York also a designer with a sewing machine? I hadn't a clue, but I did know I'd seen some long, flowing garments in Topman before, having averted my eyes to more moderate options. It was time to revisit and take a deliberate risk.

I took the escalator down to the bottom floor. There they were, shawls and wraps and other sorts of wispy, silky items. In the solitude of the fitting room, I slipped an oversized, draping shirt over my head. I checked myself out in the mirror and felt like the world's biggest idiot. My body, wide shouldered and fatally masculine, felt clunky and incorrect in the delicate garment. There was no beauty, no exciting imagined future for me to step into—going to the club, going back to HoMo, sitting down for drinks; there was none of that delicious illustration in it. There was just me: a thick, hairy man with a sweaty back in a witchy slip, playing dress-up. People would look at me, and they would laugh.

I still bought it.

I hoped that the daring act of buying it would change something in me, bring me closer to the kind of person who bought these sorts of clothes and then wore them. It would take time, I told myself, to undo everything I thought I knew. I was a gay writer in New York. I knew all the rhetoric—"internalized homophobia," "toxic masculinity"—I knew I'd supposedly been stewing in these concepts my whole life and that my thoughts had been shaped by them. I knew that looking at my bigger body as inherently masculine was a problem. I knew that the fear I felt while wearing something feminine came from the stigma of all things feminine. But knowing this didn't help. It didn't change the way I reacted to that stupid article of clothing, the way it felt like the shirt itself wanted nothing to do with me.

The blousy top stayed in its bag in my closet for weeks, shaming me with its disuse. Invitations for more parties came and went, and sometimes I did go, but I always fell back into my comfort zone of the harness. I admonished myself every time, telling myself that at some point, I would have to stop caring what other people thought. But walking to the parties with my roommate, who was always wearing something extravagant and had a face full of makeup, watching the way people reacted to him, I wondered if I would ever marshal the courage.

Unsafe. I discovered, Boring, that what I felt was unsafe. People's glances made me feel unsafe. I knew the capacity for violence that lurked behind people's eyes. I knew it from middle school, where I'd let people bully me out of my own existence. I would look at myself through their eyes sometimes, scanning for openings, a preemptive measure, no doubt. I would look at myself with their gaze, and what I saw held language, not words, really, but language—*You are wrong. You are pathetic. You are deserving of judgment and violence.*

I'd developed this lens as a means of protecting myself, Boring. Both as a fat kid and as a closeted young gay person, I developed a relationship with the space around me that was inherently adversarial. My job was to minimize the space I took up, as space was just real estate where violence could land—fat jokes, gay jokes, general punishment. It was better, always better, to shrink, to be small in appearance and in nature, to be as little as I could to give people fewer chances.

I'd shaped myself to accommodate this gaze, this eye that lived in my head and was constantly looking: within myself for errors and then without for potential threats. I would walk quicker if a rambunctious crowd of men was approaching. I would take off my jewelry and slip it in my backpack if I was walking home at night. I would go everywhere with my earphones in and my head held down, hoping no one would look at me, because being looked at was a vulnerable thing, an invitation. I was a walking statement, and I thought it prudent to, as best as I could manage, say as little as possible.

And yet, here in New York was a community, a whole world, where being loud was a virtue. I wanted desperately to join their conversation.

Even if I gathered up the courage to wear something gayer, Boring, my body would still be wrong. The beautiful people who wore these extravagant looks were thin, lithe gazelles. Then there were the men who wore next to nothing, who could just show up in jockstraps and eye shadow. They were muscular and impossibly fit. Why would I even bother adorning a body like mine, a body that wasn't distinct in any laudable way?

"Fabulous," my mother used to say when she found an outfit she particularly liked. My mom had this regal way of walking, her heels clacking from a mile away. When I think of power, that nebulous concept, I think of that sound. I would imagine what it might be like to embody it, to make a sound like that myself, to have people know when I was coming.

Fashion is a lexicon, Boring. It's a storytelling technique. Everything holds a message. Everything has something to say about the world we live in—and I found that, in the way I was dressing, in the way I was presenting, I wasn't speaking my mind. I was apologizing. I was tired of that. I wanted to feel powerful in the way that I defined power. I wanted to be like my mom clomping down the hall in heels. I wanted to be like the queers at HoMo, audacious but in my own way.

It wasn't so much clothing itself I wanted, an unmet desire to "buy stuff." It was a mode of being that I sought: a freer method of movement.

Being gay, queer, or whatever you'd like to call yourself doesn't have a uniform. There's no such thing, I've found, as "dressing gayer" or "looking gayer." You don't have to dye your hair or paint your nails. It's more important to interrogate the gaze with which you behold yourself. Whose gaze is it, and what is it looking for, Boring? What might it be like to have a lens that is more your own?

It's not about buying things or reducing queerness to commercial goods, or even down to aesthetics. It's about the relationship between presentation and identity, recognizing that our bodies exist in conversation with the world and asserting autonomy over what we're saying in it, even against the threat of violence. I found that in other forms of speech, in my writing, for example, I had no problem speaking up for myself and for others. I can only imagine what it might have been like if, in those glossy pages of *Vogue*, I had seen anything approaching the visions of myself that I held close and secret. I wish that, through visuals, someone had communicated that it was okay for me just to think about myself that way, not even necessarily to *be* that way, but to merely expand my horizons. I think that's why it's important that we express ourselves: you never know who might be listening and who needs to hear you.

Expression, be it verbal or nonverbal, is how we articulate ourselves to the world. It can bring us into closer alignment with the complexity of our interiors, which are too great and too confusing to ever be brought entirely under the sovereignty of language. But in trying, it can help us make connections. At least, thinking that way made me feel better about blowing over $100 on this beautiful linen top. It doesn't have a collar, Boring. Isn't that cool? It's like a robe I can wear outside. I discover new possibilities every day.

¡Hola Papi!

Something bad happened to me.
Can I be mad about it like . . . years later?

Signed,
Indecisive

How to Disagree with Who You Used to Be

It was a slate-gray afternoon in April, one of the many afternoons I threw down the drain in an attempt to write something, anything, while sitting empty-headed in the coffee shop near my apartment. It was the first year I'd really felt comfortable in New York, and by that I mean I could buy fancy snacks at the grocery store without having a panic attack.

Chronologically speaking, Carlos was roughly four lifetimes ago. But he, of all people, had sent me a Facebook message. This was bizarre for a few reasons, Indecisive, the first being that we hadn't spoken in years.

The second being that he was one of those people who ought to be confined to the past, if for no other reason than they'd been utterly forgotten and shouldn't assert themselves into any kind of contemporary context, as a matter of courtesy. The third being, well, how dare he?

"Hey, how have you been?" he asked, punctuation and all,

because that's fundamentally who Carlos was—drearily formal, even when he didn't have to be. I was cranky enough as it was, having sat at the coffee shop with my long-emptied cup confronting my lack of talent for the past hour or so. I considered being rude to him to let off some steam. Few people in my life deserved it like Carlos did. I might as well teach him a lesson.

But first, I should explain.

Tragedy brought Carlos and me together. I was a senior at the University of Oklahoma at the time, two years after a gay teen's suicide made national headlines. The city of Norman (and therefore, the university) had ramped up support for the local LGBTQ community in the form of resource groups and counseling. I found myself in one of these informal groups with Carlos because I was gay and suicidal and my therapist all but forced me.

In a tiled room in a church with little paper coffee cups and folding chairs arranged in a circle, we troubled queers sat down and met for the first time. A chic, silver-haired woman with a southern drawl and a placid, almost sleepy expression on her face was our counselor. She introduced herself as Martha in a voice that kept us at a respectful distance, as if we were soufflés that might collapse if she wasn't careful. "Why don't we meet one another? Give me your name, what you're studying, and a fun fact."

I gave my name, said I was studying professional writing, which, I always felt compelled to add, was a sort of bastard child of the journalism school and the English department. My fun fact was that I was left-handed, the answer I always gave when asked for a fun fact because I didn't believe any fact about me could be "fun."

Next was Carlos. He wore glasses and a neat wool sweater over a gingham shirt tucked into his slacks. His hair was black and curly and his hands were folded in his lap. He was staring off somewhere that wasn't here. "Oh, sorry," he said, all whimsical. "My name is Carlos. I'm studying French. A fun fact about me is that I can wiggle my ears." He did not demonstrate.

There was a rule to our group, Martha told us. We were not to meet up outside of it. Once group was concluded at the end of the semester we could hang out if we so chose, but things could get awkward quickly if we formed cliques or, God forbid, hooked up while we were sharing traumas together every week. I found it pretty easy to adhere to this rule as I'd immediately decided no one there was my type. I received a few friend requests and Grindr messages and flirtations from my new colleagues, but I always shrugged them off. If anything, the group was a good excuse not to have to talk to them outside its sacred confines.

Carlos made no such attempts with me; in the thoughts I imagined him having, he considered himself above all this and was at most amused by our collective insistence that our feelings mattered. As the weeks went by, he was the one who shared the least, always pivoting from the big questions. "I guess I have trouble sleeping," he'd say, or, "Sometimes I find it difficult to focus." So it surprised me when he stopped me on my way out of the church after one session. "Hey," he said, breathless, like he'd been suppressing it until this very moment. "Would you like to get coffee with me?"

I didn't find Carlos very attractive, Indecisive. He was like a bespectacled owl to me, like the Tootsie Pop owl wearing a graduation cap. What I did like was the way he carried himself. He wasn't confident, per se, but he was worldly. He seemed traveled, like he had seen things altogether more interesting than here, than me. I found myself wanting to be, in his view, a sight.

"Sure," I said. "Uh, now?"

Over hot chocolate at Starbucks I learned that Carlos was studying French literature, specifically. He'd been to France several times and he said he liked the bread, and that American bread was too soft and sweet.

"To be honest with you, the bread here is shit," he said. "It should be classified as, like, I don't know, some kind of sad dessert."

It was the first time I'd seen him passionate about anything, and I was titillated by his sudden lurch into emotion—something I'd assumed he'd found ridiculous about the rest of us.

"I was in Marseille for six months," he clarified, whipped cream on the edge of his mouth. He had this way of pronouncing French words, all syrupy and authentic. "I'm probably going to Lyon next, but I really want to stay in a small village if I can. I want to ride a bike every day."

I didn't have much to go on compared to Carlos. Though I was well traveled thanks to my parents, I'd never lived abroad. Carlos was accustomed to spending long periods of time in the places he went, making friends who'd drink wine with him in the park and have picnics, cooking for each other and sharing their lives. "I haven't decided where I want to go," I lied. "Maybe to Spain since I speak Spanish, kind of."

We said goodbye in the parking lot, him looking pleased, me feeling frustrated because our conversation had sparked feelings of inadequacy and a sense that I'd failed to impress, which I carried into our next group sessions.

In one session, we all argued about religion. Someone said that gay people "hating on Christians" was just as bad as Christians hating gay people. I said those two things were nowhere near the same, as only one had any real power to drive someone to hating themselves or to closeting themselves. "I like what J. P. said," Carlos added. I found myself chasing those moments of validation from him whenever I spoke, which was definitely not supposed to be the point of group therapy.

And then, Valentine's Day came. "Hello," Carlos texted. "I was just wondering what your plans were this Thursday. Let me know?" When I told him I was free, he responded, "Oh, wow. I didn't know it was Valentine's Day. I want to meet up, but there's no pressure if that makes it weird for you." We agreed to make dinner at his place. Was this a date? If so, I wished he'd just said so instead of hedging as he had. I may not have known what I wanted, Indecisive, but I was pretty sure I didn't want someone who also didn't know what he wanted.

We picked a Julia Child recipe at random—fish in white sauce with vegetables. We drove to Target to pick up the ingredients; I hated the way Carlos drove, his hands fidgeting on the wheel, swerving constantly. I started getting carsick with each jerk of the brake.

Whenever an ingredient proved difficult to track down, Carlos would say, "It's fine! We can skip that part. All good." This irritated me, as I figured skipping any one part of the recipe, no matter how small and frivolous it might seem, would screw everything up. I found myself tallying his flaws, building a case against him, but nevertheless persisting.

We cooked in Carlos's empty house in a cookie-cutter neighborhood in Norman. We'd followed the recipe as best we could, missing a little something here and a little something there, and the result was a goopy white mess that looked like it might gain sentience at any moment and let out a burp.

"It will taste good," Carlos offered. It did not.

So why did I keep going, Indecisive? Why, when he poured us two glasses of wine and we sat at a card table with a tablecloth and lit candles, did I do my best to conjure what I liked about Carlos? I thought about how dignified he made me feel, how he offered me glimpses of some other kind of life where people spoke foreign languages and talked about books I hadn't read. In the soft warm light, I rooted for him and against my intuition.

A wise person might surmise that perhaps Carlos and I were incompatible, given how often I was irritated with him. But I perceived my irritation, rather, as a character flaw in myself, a roadblock I had to overcome if I was ever to end up with someone as good as Carlos.

He held his wineglass in two hands, laughing, with a scrunched-up face and flushed cheeks. There was a flicker of desire for him, suddenly, and what we might look like together.

As the meal ended, he asked, as if he hadn't been waiting to ask it, "Would you like to go lie down for a bit?" I went willingly, holding that flicker in my heart, trying to stoke the embers.

We lay side by side on his bed in his unkempt room with fat books strewn about and an ironing board with a hill of wrinkled clothes heaped on it. The room was nothing like Carlos, who never had a hair out of place, his clothes always pressed neatly. But this was his room, and this was Carlos; this was him, too. I held on to this—perhaps I didn't know people as well as I thought I did and Carlos could still surprise me.

He threw an arm over my chest, as if he were asleep and just happened to roll over like that. Everything he did was so cautious, hedged, and felt more like a probe into seeing how I would react than a genuine move on its own.

I stroked his arm with my hand, stubbornly unwilling to initiate anything. It was as though he'd left me to complete chores in a house where I didn't live. He began moving his arm back and forth over my chest, like a windshield wiper. I sighed, pulled him on top of me, and he quickly took his glasses off and plunged his face into mine.

I'd been told some people were bad kissers, Indecisive, but I don't think I'd actually really met any until Carlos, whose kisses were small and pecking and yet, somehow, too wet, even though he wasn't using his tongue. He planted these on me in random places, my cheek, my hand, my lips, and my neck, little, doting pecks all over me that I hated. I kissed him back just to localize his attempts to my lips. He reared back and took his shirt off, revealing a soft, fuzzy body with a paunch belly. He took off his pants next, and I dutifully did the same until we were both naked. He began to lurch on top of me, rubbing up and down against me. I closed my eyes because I thought it looked a little silly, but all the while I was chastising myself: *Be kinder, be gentler, be more patient.*

It mercifully ended. We stared at the ceiling. I didn't typically feel ashamed after hooking up, but this time felt desperately inappropriate, if for no other reason than I hadn't really felt like doing it but had done it anyway.

"You have a lot of books," I said, attempting to meander into conversation.

"Oh, yes," Carlos said. He often spoke like this, as if apologetic. "You know, I can't read most of them on the first try, the French ones. I have to read them once, then again to pick out the words I struggle with, and the third time I usually get it."

"That sounds like torture," I said.

"I guess it kind of is."

I mentioned something to Carlos about not wanting to go back to my family's house in Cache for the summer, and he quickly offered that his roommate would be gone until next year. I could stay in his room and not have to pay anything.

"Wow, are you sure?" I asked.

"Oh, definitely, definitely," Carlos said, as if it were the most obvious thing, but failing to mask his eagerness. "I will be so bored without someone else here."

I could pretend I didn't know any better, that I was naïve, that I was too young, too freshly out of the closet to avoid these kinds of mistakes. But that's not true. It wasn't false consciousness, a misunderstanding of myself that led me to move in with Carlos. Because the truth is I did have my appetites, even if they were in conflict—hunger for worship, for being wanted. And in some shadowy corner of my mind I did want to be undone, wanted to punish myself, wanted to subdue my restless passions—for adventure, for men, for more, more, always more than I had—with Carlos as my reckoning. I wanted Carlos to want me, even if I saw wanting me as a desperate, unattractive thing.

My room was bare: four white walls, a window into the small yard, a beige carpeted floor, and a bed with a white comforter. I didn't have much to bring with me other than a suitcase with my clothes.

I quickly fell into a numbing routine. I'd look for odd jobs during the day, waste time at the coffee shop staring at a blank Word document, go for a run, and wait for Carlos to come home from his job as a cashier at the organic grocery store. Within weeks, I felt like a ghost, whiling my day away in Carlos's empty house.

Carlos had started a strange ritual of coming home at night, finding me on my bed, and collapsing onto me, exhausted from his day. Oddly enough, Indecisive, I enjoyed this. Acting out this domestic role as Carlos's support at home was something to do. I could play house until it was time to go to Barcelona in August, plans I had firmed up just before graduating. I had taken to some bad habits, waking up at noon and going to bed early. I was beginning to feel like I was losing my mind. Late one afternoon I threw the book I was reading across the room at the wall, hoping it would provoke some emotion in me. It didn't. So, I cleaned. I cooked. I tried to use domesticity to fend off what felt like the end of my being, a suffocating numbness that was threatening to swallow me up.

On some evenings, Carlos and I would go out to eat, though we were both low on cash. At a campus spot called the Mont, a sort of tavern with bar eats and frozen sugary drinks with names like "the Sooner Swirl," we discussed the state of our lives together.

"I guess I feel nothing," I said. "It's kind of scary. I don't think I can write anymore. I'm trying every day, but I can't."

"It will come back," Carlos said, trying to reassure me. Who was this person? Why was I in his house, and why was he always crawling into bed with me? It was his bed, I supposed. But then, why was I in it?

I was me; Carlos was Carlos; this was all temporary. These facts were becoming clearer as I inched toward Barcelona.

But I'd be lying if I said I didn't care about him, Indecisive. There was some part of him that I liked and felt warmth for and flirted with every day to see if I could coax it out, that same flicker I'd glimpsed on Valentine's Day—him laughing sitting at the card table, holding his wineglass in both hands, knowing so much about the world that I didn't, and yet, still choosing me.

Then I got sick.

When I say I got sick, Indecisive, I don't mean with a cold or with something that kept me in bed for a couple of days. This sickness came on like an apocalypse: brain-splitting, blinding pain that lit up my body followed by periods of sweaty numbness. I wailed and moaned, I tossed and turned, I cried.

I had no idea what I had come down with. I suppose it could have been the flu, but I'd had the flu before and it hadn't felt like this. I entertained the idea that I might die. It was in this state that Carlos came home from work to find me one evening. "Jesus," he said, kneeling beside my soaked bed to get a closer look. "What's going on?"

"*Hnnngggg...*," I moaned.

"Do you want a bath?" Carlos asked after some time. "I'll start you a bath, okay?"

Through the fog of my pain, I must admit it felt good to be cared for by Carlos. I'd never really had someone who wasn't a relative take any great interest in my well-being. It was a new phenomenon, and new from Carlos, who broke his reticent demeanor to become my nurse, urgent and emphatic. He carefully guided me to the bathroom in his room, where he'd made me a hot bath. He undressed me gingerly, as if I might unravel if he removed something too quickly. He lowered me into the scalding water, where I sat limp and groaning.

What happened next came on slowly. It unfolded through the stabbing blows of fever; I still had the good sense to be unsettled. Carlos began taking his clothes off, too. He removed them quickly, as if seizing on some narrow window of opportunity that might slam shut at any moment, and climbed in behind me.

I froze, not knowing how to react. I didn't know if I could react at all, being as weak as I was. He began washing me with a cloth, his erection pressed to my back.

I resented the idea of someone's touch lingering on me for the rest of my life. The touch I experienced in the tub was like that—his penis, so intrusive, so unwanted, so hated, left such a distinct physical sensation on me. It was like I knew all at once, even on the brink of passing out from my illness, how long this touch would stay with me, how difficult if not entirely impossible it would be to scrub out, and so I, exhausted by the idea, chose instead to ignore it because I hadn't asked for it, didn't want it, and it had nothing to give me but anger. I told myself I would leave this in the water.

The next day, my mom and sister came to pick me up. I'd sent my sister a desperate text saying I was extremely sick, and they'd decided to come up and collect me. We packed up my sparse belongings, Carlos looking on with mute culpability. I gave him my anemic goodbye and went back to Cache to recover until it was time to leave for Barcelona.

It was in Barcelona, in a cramped flat where I was staying with four frat boys who'd keep me up late into the night with their partying and their fighting with shifty new friends (they partied and fought in roughly equal measure), that Carlos called me. It was two in the morning, but I was awake.

He went right into it. "I've made up my mind. I don't want to go to France. I want to stay here with you."

"Here?" I asked, drowsily triangulating myself on the globe. "Uh, *here* here?"

"No, sorry," Carlos clarified. "I mean Oklahoma. When you come back, I want to be together."

"Okay, so," I began, "don't *not* go to France for me. That's dumb. You should go to France."

"I should?" He sounded hurt.

"France is your whole thing," I said. "Is it not?"

"Well, yes," he said, and paused before continuing. "But you're worth it to me. You matter more than France." I winced a little.

It might sound wild that I'd even entertain the idea, Indecisive. But I was having trouble making friends in Barcelona, I felt isolated, and I'd never had a real boyfriend before. I found myself having unexpected pangs of nostalgia for Carlos's house, which I had hated—the asphalt streets, the simple room with its oppressive blank walls. I missed them, I guess because I knew them, and that's all nostalgia really requires of us.

But the other thing, the big thing, was that I felt Carlos held the power to define me. I still didn't have a clear notion of who I was. I held fragments, but they never quite cohered into a singular vision. Carlos had a vision of who I was, and liked it enough to rearrange his life around it. Should I not nurture that vision, as one might a garden? I told Carlos he should go to France, but I also told him I was excited to see him when I got back.

Carlos relented, but he had a proposal. He had to go to Houston to get his visa from the French consulate in person; so, why don't I come with him to meet his parents in Tulsa, hang out for a bit, and then do a road trip to Houston together? "As friends," he said. "No pressure or anything. It would just be a fun thing."

I didn't have much else to do. I was looking for jobs, but no matter what path I chose, I had a long, boring grind ahead of me. Why not lurch into chaos—yet another road trip to Texas—because, what could possibly go wrong?

Studying abroad hadn't opened my horizons as I'd hoped. It had instead confirmed some of my nagging fears: that I had trouble connecting with people and making friends, and that happiness probably lay in the familiar, in the things I knew, even if I found most familiar things to be dull. I thought perhaps my problem was my lack of devotion, my childish insistence that love and work and the big things in life ought to be spectacular and not, more astutely, daily chores.

I came back to Oklahoma ready to settle. A few weeks after coming back home, I rolled up to a beautiful house in a leafy neighborhood in Tulsa, the kind with shiny Range Rovers parked out on the curb, for fear of nothing. Carlos greeted me in the driveway wearing pastel shorts and a loose, casual tee, an outfit I'd never seen him in before. "Hey!" he said, bright and cheerful.

"Hey!" I said, shrugging off my bag to hug him. He even felt warmer. Had something changed since I'd seen him last, or was it the new setting?

Both of Carlos's parents were doctors. His dad was at work, but his mom, an elegant woman wearing a smart white blazer with thick black hair just above her shoulders, floated over to me. "John Paul," she said with an airy affection I always imagined educated rich people to have, the kind who traveled and knew obscure facts. "Carlos has told me so much about you. How was Barcelona?"

Barcelona had sucked. But I mentioned the highlights: the museum of modern art, the Botero sculpture in El Raval, the food. "It's a heck of a lot of tomatoes and cured meat, isn't it?" she said, before adding, "That's a party city." She winked. "So how was it *really*?"

I'd never met a mom like this.

I ended up getting along with Carlos's mom much better than I did with Carlos. I considered actually dating him again just to be around her more. "Now, I have to ask you," she said as if she were letting me into some secret club. "It's an important question, but try not to think about it too hard, okay? Here goes. Steinbeck. Yes or no?"

"Yes," I offered immediately, not because I was a Steinbeck fan or anything, but because Steinbeck was one of those writers one just said yes to, him being taught in schools and all. I'd read *The Grapes of Wrath*, anyway.

"Yes!" she said, and then turned to Carlos approvingly. "That's the right answer. Thank goodness. He can stay." Despite only accidentally offering the correct answer, I nevertheless felt embraced by this impressive woman, recognized as kindred.

We had dinner that night at an upscale Mexican restaurant with Carlos's dad, who looked remarkably like the person I'd picture when talking about "a man of letters": glasses, a scholarly baldness, a tweed jacket. He seemed tired in that intelligent, affable way. "Gosh, John Paul, it's good to have you," he said over margaritas, another taboo broken: absolutely no one in my family drank, and seeing a parent be so flagrant about it was like being a tourist all over again. "Carlos tells me you write. What about?"

Strictly speaking I wasn't writing anything. I bumbled through assignments, short stories and screenplays and such, and sometimes I'd try my hand at Tumblr fame by writing brief, overwrought poems in a typewriter font in Photoshop. Writing, as a nebulous concept, was more about my certainty that there were good, worthy thoughts rattling around in my brain somewhere and my life's mission ought to be to fish them out by hook or by crook. So far, it hadn't been going well.

"I wrote a screenplay recently," I said. "It was kind of about Mexico, but mostly it was about a family. It won first place in this thing I entered." I immediately regretted adding that last part. It was true, my screenplay had won first place in a campus film festival competition. As a prize I'd been given Final Draft, the fancy screenwriting software. But saying so was tacky, a sad, naked attempt at impressing these people. Writers who were good, *actually* good, were so bored with their own talent that they didn't think about it much or have to talk about it, I was certain.

"Well, hey," Carlos's dad said, genuinely intrigued. "That's something. I was a bit of a writer myself for a while. Couldn't write a screenplay, I'll tell you that. Everything has to be so succinct. It takes me a few hundred words to clear my throat."

"You've got to believe him," Carlos's mom said with exaggerated disgust. "I used to read his stuff in college. John Paul, you would not believe . . ."

"She's exposing me for a hack," he laughed. "It's her favorite pastime."

It wasn't that I never talked about writing or the specifics of my life with my own family. My mom had been my English teacher during freshman year of high school, a role I didn't have much trouble adjusting to because she'd always been exacting at home. She was great at homing in on what was wrong—the grammar here, the structure there. My dad didn't say much in general. All of this was fine to me. I didn't see parents as people you needed to share the embarrassing dimensions of your hobbies with, and I'd never thought to try. But Carlos's parents offered a new dynamic—one where parents and children drank and discussed creative exploits, together. I wanted that. I wondered if Carlos could give it to me.

For his part, Carlos sat askew from the conversation. He seemed to have relinquished a readiness to intervene if necessary. Things were going well. In fact, I felt better about Carlos then than I had in a long time. Somehow, putting him in context with his parents, in proximity to these luminous adults, made him seem like a better idea.

That night, back at his house, Carlos's mom offered us a shot of bourbon. I hated shots, but I took it because in my mind I could weasel my way into becoming her son if I kept choosing correctly: Steinbeck, bourbon, what next? It was a matter of taking the right steps.

We cuddled up in Carlos's bed and watched a movie. He didn't try to do anything more and I wondered if he knew that this was the way to win me over: to not try so much. I wanted it to be possible, Indecisive. I thought that if I could just love Carlos, if my big dumb brain could *just love Carlos*, this *one* person, then I could materialize this life. I could get to know his parents. I could read more books. I could become a part of this shiny family, and we could drink and be merry together. We fell asleep with the TV on, and in the morning we set out for Houston.

Then came the unraveling.

It was about an eight-hour drive from Tulsa to Houston. Per usual, I got carsick with Carlos behind the wheel, but I was quicker to forgive him this time with his parents still fresh in my mind. We filled the dead space, the long spans of silence, with the radio: an evangelical program we could scoff at, on-air miracles and breathless declarations of faith. When I quickly got bored, I started keeping an eye out for road signs, words and letters of any kind I could arrange and rearrange in my head, "shop" becoming "posh" and so on.

Houston at last came into view like a blessing, sprawling and mysterious.

"I was thinking we could drop off our stuff at the hotel and explore a bit," Carlos said. It turned out the hotel was inside a mall, which seemed incredibly perverse to me—who would sleep in a mall? But nonetheless we carried our small bags through the crowded Galleria and set up camp in the attached Hyatt. "Well," Carlos said, irritated, I thought, but at what? "Let's explore."

We found a gay club called South Beach that was drenched in purple light and deafening pop. It was not the sort of place I'd ever have associated with Carlos, but there we were. I was tired from the long drive, enchanted as I was by the club—I always got a kick out of knowing that in cities all over the world there were gays with their familiar haunts. "South Beach?" their texts might read to their friends every Friday.

Carlos bought us mixed drinks, and then another round. Awkward as ever, he tried to dance on me. There it was again, my familiar contempt for him bubbling up as he tried to hump my leg like a horny Chihuahua. I sipped my drink, hoping to get drunk faster, and Carlos yanked my face toward his and kissed me.

It was a reflex to pull away. Carlos tried to pull my face back in, but again I turned away. He shoved me then, spilling some of my drink on my feet. The people near us strategically angled their gaze to catch an argument. I stood shocked, unwilling to accept what had just happened. "Fuck this," Carlos said, then marched away.

I followed him, pushing past people dancing and laughing and drinking, outside into the parking lot.

"Where are you going?" I asked.

He wheeled on me. "You know when you look at other guys?"

he said, a feral expression on his face. "It makes me want to punch you."

"Punch me?"

He turned to the car. "Either you get in now or I'm leaving you here," he said.

I got in.

I couldn't think of anything to say. Everything was ringing.

Carlos drove at an alarming speed. He took us up the overpass. "I should just fucking drive us off this," he said, and I failed myself for the umpteenth time by merely closing my eyes and waiting— perhaps there would be the feeling of flying, perilous, and then a violent smash, and then nothing. When I was little, my abuelo would drive my cousins and me down a certain hill in Wichita Falls as fast as he could, and for a second we were lifted out of our seats. I thought of that, clung to the comfort of that memory, and assured myself it would feel the same.

He didn't drive us off the overpass. We arrived back at the mall Hyatt, where he kicked his shoes off against the wall and turned to me. "Tell me what you fucking want," he said. "Tell me right now. Do you love me?"

How odd, I thought, how unfair, that he would ask it that way. *Do you love me?* I didn't know what it meant to love anybody. I wanted good things for a lot of people. I would go out of my way for quite a few people. There were many people, like Carlos, whom I didn't want to hurt—a kind of love, I suppose. But I knew what kind of love Carlos was talking about: love of the involuntary, overwhelming sort, the kind, I figured, he felt for me.

"No," I said after a beat, and it landed on Carlos, I could see, I could tell, like a burlap sack of nails. I had to close the door behind me after spending months in the entryway, Indecisive. It felt good, or at least final.

But here a new problem arose: we were stuck together.

"I'm going to jump off," he told me, making his way to the balcony.

"Carlos," I said sternly. "No. Don't jump off. Okay? Don't."

He started howling. He threw his glasses aside, buried his face in his hands, and bawled. "Fuck you!" he said. Then, "I'm going to fucking punch you."

"And then what?" I asked, keenly aware that I was much bigger. Caught, he instead fished his phone out of his pocket and called someone. "Mom?" he said, and my blood rushed down to my feet. He walked out into the hallway, slamming the door behind him, but I could hear most of what he was saying: *He's horrible. I can't believe this. He's fucking horrible. What do I do? What can I do?* Then a long pause, where his mother's advice must have been, and he said, "Nietzsche," with eager agreement, and I wondered, would long wonder, what quote from Nietzsche could possibly have suited this situation.

He came back inside, eyes red and veiny. We met each other's gaze for a while, and then he went and lay down on his bed.

He would break the silence with infrequent jabs: "You're not going to find anyone better than me," he spat. "You never will." Then, "You're going to be miserable forever. You'll never have anyone love you."

And then, at last and for the first time in years, I wept. I wept and wept and wept until I coughed, until my vision went blurry, not caring anymore about how this person would perceive me. I felt I was being fitfully freed, relief that it would soon be over, pain that it was being so torturously drawn out.

We went on like this, spikes and fits of emotion and temporary lulls. How misplaced these conversations were; a moment where we agreed dating was harder for us because we were mentally ill, a moment where we apologized, a moment where he asked me, as if he knew he had forfeited being the adult in the room, "What's wrong with me?"

But these are wispy, errant things compared to the overpass, the balcony, the phone call where he took a hammer to my imagined closeness with his mother; *Nietzsche.* When did he get his visa? It must have happened at some point. But my mind has muddled the rest of that trip, save that night, and the following morning when I sheepishly climbed into the passenger seat of his car.

On the long drive home, to my astonishment, Carlos began to perk up. He started talking again. He told me he didn't really want to study French literature anymore. He wanted to study medicine, like his parents. He was excited to let them know this, and our going back to Tulsa became a sort of quest to deliver a big gift to his mom and dad. Dizzy and all but empty, I smiled, eager to encourage this train of thought: "That's great. Is that what they wanted you to do? Oh, good."

Upon arriving, Carlos's mom enveloped him in her arms, an acknowledgment, I thought, of the pain I'd inflicted on her son and her eagerness to make it right. I knew there would be no more warmth for me. Kindness and courtesy, yes, and I had no doubt she would show it, her being the kind of woman she was. But I knew any idea of closeness was shattered. I felt I had been tipped over and poured out.

His parents called for a meeting between the four of us that night, and out of obligation to parents of any kind I agreed, rather than just fleeing. I still carried in my bones the Catholic notion of atonement—that if I had erred, which I believed I had, then I ought to endure the consequences if I was ever to cleanse myself.

In their living room, they solemnly set themselves down on the couch, Carlos and I sitting opposite them. "John Paul," his mother said, her eyes soft and sorry, not apologetic, but sorry, as if things could have gone differently and that was too bad. "I just want you to know that we know . . . what happened with you and Carlos, and we don't want you to feel uncomfortable in our house. Okay? You're more than welcome here, and I know Carlos feels the same way." Carlos eagerly nodded.

"That's good to hear," I said, feigning relief. "That's so good to hear. Thank you."

"I have something to say, too," Carlos said, perhaps eager to move this part along. "Mom, Dad, I've given it a lot of thought, and I know I've been going down this path for a while so it might take some major adjusting, but I've decided I want to pursue medicine."

"Oh?" Carlos's dad, who'd been sitting with his arms crossed on the couch, perked up as if Carlos had just announced there was a grandbaby on the way. "You have?"

"Yes," Carlos said, eyes dancing.

"Well, Carl"—his mother beamed, using a new name I hadn't heard for him—"that's just . . . Oh, Carl." She was on the verge of tears. Carlos smiled bigger and wider than I'd ever seen before.

They embraced, and I wanted, for the first time in all this, to sock him.

Of course, I would not be spending the night with Carlos in his room, but it was late, I was deathly tired, and the journey back to Cache was too long to face that evening. I would be staying in the guest room, which used to be his older sister's. She, too, was a doctor. The room was a pink, frilly affair, with an abundance of pillows and stuffed animals. I fell asleep almost immediately, a deeper sleep than I've had before or since. In the early hours of dawn, I heard Carlos downstairs, playing the piano and singing, his illusion bidding me goodbye—the Carlos who read lots of books, knew things about the world I didn't know, who played instruments and understood sheet music and might, just might, if I played my cards correctly, take me along. There was never such a person to begin with. There had always, and only, been Carlos.

I drifted back to sleep, and the next time I stirred was when I realized someone was climbing into bed with me, underneath the lacy blanket, situating their body behind mine. Then, a shift, and the person was rubbing my feet, massaging them. It was Carlos.

He massaged my feet with his clammy hands and then resettled next to me. He pulled me close to him, pushed his erection up against my back, and whispered in my ear, his breath bearing down on my cheek. "I love you," he said. "I will always love you. You don't have to love me back. You don't have to do anything at all. Just let me love you, John Paul. Let me love you."

I don't remember his letting me go. Why didn't I push him off? Why didn't I pretend to be asleep? I have no answers; I haven't sought them out, either. I don't remember how, but at some point I made it to my car and drove away. It seems to me now, Indecisive, to be some act of herculean strength, climbing into my car and driving all those hours back to Cache. What was I thinking that whole time? I must have known something bad had happened; I was panicked enough to log on to the Twitter account I hadn't used in months and tweet, "I think I was just sexually assaulted," but deleted it when it actually drew replies.

Not every dilemma gets consciously resolved, Indecisive. I'd like to say I put in work and overcame what happened to me in Carlos's house. But the reality is, I merely kept living until it was buried. I couldn't think of it then the way I do now.

Years went by. I moved to DC, and then to New York, and I didn't think much of Carlos. I considered myself to be a different person entirely back then, navigating a context that would seem utterly alien to me now, my previous woes inaccessible—remember driving a car? Remember not having a job?

I was excellent at banishing that self away; I'd built a new world for a new me to inhabit. And that was when his message came, while I was sitting in the coffee shop.

"Hey, how have you been?"

It was then that I scrolled up and saw that this wasn't the first time he'd messaged me since we'd parted ways. He'd done so before, four years prior, when I'd lived in DC. "Hey J. P.," he had said. "How are you?" And to my horror I saw that I'd responded: "Hey Carlos! I'm good, just busy with work. How about you?"

There was a whole conversation—nothing deep, nothing much

beyond friendly small talk, but it was friendly nonetheless. It was kind. It was like nothing bad had happened at all. I hated myself more than I hated him in that chat. Didn't I know? Didn't I care about what had happened to me?

I walked into the coffee shop bathroom, thinking I might throw up. The memories were flooding back, yes, but worse than that was the betrayal. Why, why had I been kind to him?

I heaved but didn't vomit. I felt the urge to hit myself, punishment for what I had just seen and subjected myself to.

I had never wanted to claim any of what had happened between Carlos and me as "mine." Our Valentine's Day dinner had been his idea; our trip to Houston, his idea; what he'd done to me when I was sick, when I was in his parents' home—that was his. I didn't want something so ugly in my hands.

But then, it hadn't been just him; recognizing that wasn't the same as blaming myself or absolving Carlos. I had wanted his approval. I had wanted his affection. I had kept placing myself in his orbit, because I'd wanted to see myself there. And perhaps that realization could help me see more of the situation as mine, as something that did have a lot to do with me, and something I could forgive myself for.

My experience of those events was mine. My point of view, my coping, that all belonged to me. So wasn't it fine, wasn't it expected, then, that my approach to it might change over time as I had changed?

The facts as I recalled them were the same. But the way I arranged them, the story I made out of them, had shifted. It was only later in the café that I realized my forgotten exchange with

Carlos had taken place before a period of public reckoning for people who'd experienced sexual assault: every week was a new story about an abuse of power, an unwanted advance, a time to reconsider the past and whether or not we were okay with it.

That period, even without my knowing it, must have changed the way I thought about my experience. What was wrong about that?

My previous exchange with Carlos, on the surface, looked friendly enough, and would look that way to any third-party observer. But I knew better now. I recognized in my past self a feeling, again, of obligation. That time, it was to reply to him, just to sate him and get him out of my hair, to not have to put up with any hurt feelings or end up somewhere deeper than I needed to be. I was polite, and then I moved on. Though I no longer agree with it, it was, in its own way, a strategy. A way to keep things moving.

Looking over his new message, I chose not to respond again. I didn't block him, either. I merely closed the chat and kept on with the project of my life. It's important I think, Indecisive, to occasionally remind ourselves that we are not static beings. The version of me in that hotel room and the version of me that replied to Carlos were both me and not me, guided by different understandings and contexts and subconscious motives that maybe I'll never be able to unearth. And yet, they are me nonetheless, in the geological way the earth is layered—ancient, old, recent, new, in a gradient toward the surface.

But I, me, myself, stand at the top. And from here, with the freedom of movement it grants me, I've come to think that it's fine, and perhaps expected, to change your mind.

¡Hola Papi!

*How do I become more confident
in my identity?*

*Signed,
Imposter Syndrome*

How to Decide Who to Be

Miguel sometimes sold jewelry on the street. He rode a bike everywhere and he used to wear his hair down past his shoulders until recently, before I met him, deciding to buzz it off because hair was a needless fuss. He never stayed in one place for too long. He knew a nice spot well protected from the waves of tourists that crashed down on San José del Cabo, and he said we should meet there.

I was staying in a resort with my family. I've never liked resorts, Imposter. They reek of some agenda. My dad had won a free trip to Mexico and decided to bring his family along. I felt inappropriately large the entire time, like a teenager wading through the ball pit at Chuck E. Cheese.

The shame wasn't that I was traveling with my parents. It was that I considered myself at that time a sort of failed project: I was anxious, restless, having graduated from college just a month prior; each day meant wrestling with the unpleasant task of turning my writing degree into anything worth anyone's time. I had no direction, had next to no money, and didn't know how to explain myself. When relatives or acquaintances back in Oklahoma asked me what I was going to do, I had no answer other than to say I was tutoring and doing remote internships. The former was true, and the latter had been true up until the knitting company I was interning for had forgotten I existed entirely. I had elected not to remind them.

I knew I was supposed to do something, and that whatever it was would help me cohere into a real person. But I didn't know what it was, and so in the meanwhile I felt like no one at all.

Miguel came into the picture like a lot of men in my life did— through a dating app. This time, it was Tinder. We'd matched while my family and I were eating in a restaurant not far from a cockfighting tent where our meal was occasionally punctuated by shrieking roosters. His pictures showed him on his bike or reclining in a hammock. He was slim with black hair and furious eyebrows, an impassive look in his eyes that smacked of judgment.

The bar Miguel suggested was perched on a protruding cliff and nestled among trees. Inside were neon signs, a jukebox, and not much else, in direct protest, I thought, against the typical trappings of Cabo.

I'm not sure how it came to be that I met Miguel's acquaintances before I met him. But I do know, Imposter, that while waiting for him to arrive I found myself at a table in the bar with two girls, one dressed pinup style with winged eyeliner and a yellow bandana in her hair, the other a chic, disheveled blonde who looked like she'd rather have been napping but had deigned to appear out of charity. They worked on a luxury cruise liner.

"How do you know Miguel?" the blonde with the tired eyes asked. I told her we'd matched on Tinder. "He's great," was all she said, and I could tell by the way she said it that it was a compliment she scarcely anointed anyone with.

As if summoned, Miguel appeared in the doorway. He was taking his helmet off, and perhaps because of his stature or because he actually knew everyone there was to know in town, the whole bar seemed to acknowledge his entrance by turning their heads. "Yo," he greeted the women, looking every bit as intense as his Tinder pictures had. Pinup smiled the kind of smile people reserve for military reunions, launched from her seat, and gave him a hug. "You!" she said.

The blonde, meanwhile, smiled serenely. "Hi, baby," she said, dripping with a reproachful lust that made me wonder what had happened there. Then Miguel turned to me and, of all things, kissed me on the forehead. "This is mi novio," he told the women. "I hope you approve."

"Still deciding. I'll let you know," pinup girl said with a playful smirk. I liked the girls, who shared a funny dynamic—pinup was loud and corny, and the apathetic girl with sleepy eyes looked at her admiringly, as if pinup were a rambunctious pet of hers.

They told me about the cruise liner lifestyle, docking here and there, scurrying out, drinking, fucking, and then returning to their cots. Miguel approved of all this, it seemed, as he met their adventures with nods of his head. "That's the way to go about it," he said. He'd activate, widen his eyes or clap his hands, whenever one of the girls confessed to undoing some staple convention of being a person: having a job, getting an apartment, entering a relationship, all things they didn't do because they were living on a boat, all things Miguel agreed should be disposed of.

To me, his rejection of all things sedentary was a bit much, like a loud and blatant accessory. But I decided to roll with it. It enhanced the story for me, anyway, and one thing I was short on was stories worth telling.

Miguel asked me about my family, and I told him my mom was Mexican, which he pounced on with uncharacteristic quickness, leaning in and cocking an eyebrow.

"Oh, and what does that mean?"

"I'm not sure," I said, which was true. I didn't really think of Mexico, the place and the geographic reality, as having anything to do with me, a fact I only realized in that very moment while talking with Miguel. Mexico was abstracted in my mind, a place where my family had come from and where my culture had originated, and that was what I meant whenever I said "Mexican."

"Ah, okay," he said. "What else are you? Anything else?" It was then that I learned it wasn't the "Mexican" thing Miguel was fixated on: to him, any assertion of identity was a serious and misguided thing that needed to be interrogated until it went away. He did it to pinup, too. "What do you mean you're broke, huh? What does that mean?"

It was easy for him; he never claimed to be anything himself. He offered instead things he'd done or things that had happened to him: He'd ridden his bike all the way to Chiapas. His dad had kicked him out when he was thirteen. He had had girlfriends and boyfriends.

I felt a bit admonished, Imposter. Not by the "Mexican" thing, but by my desire to have any kind of identity at all, which in Miguel's presence now seemed frivolous and desperate. Being Mexican, being gay, these were things I had at long last decided upon after much ado, but here I felt childish for doing so, as if I weren't confident and mature enough to realize I was nothing, and couldn't be okay with being nothing.

My sense was that my evening was going poorly with Miguel, as confrontation of any kind was a bad sign in my book. But then he paid for everyone's drinks and informed the girls he'd be taking me back with him. "Mi novio the tourist. I have to watch out for him." I was relieved, as I so often was back then whenever a man, even one I wasn't hugely excited for, deigned to accept me.

We said goodbye and left the girls to their lives. Miguel walked his bike in one hand and me in the other back toward someplace—his house? It couldn't be. A friend's house, maybe? I didn't know.

"You're afraid to hold my hand in the street?" Miguel asked, although I was holding it and hadn't said anything. A truck had gone by with a man hanging off the back of it, and I suppose I had divulged some conceit to discomfort, somewhere. "Why?"

"I'm not," I said.

"You are," he said. Maybe it was the fact that Miguel had the face of a statue, never smiling or laughing or even frowning, that lent him such authority to define things, even things about me, things deep in my interior. He didn't wield this irresponsibly, I thought. He was right, after all. "You don't have to be."

He didn't know it, but as we walked on that cloudless night

through San José, which was different from San José del Cabo, the former being the more practical sibling, I fixated on that: *You don't have to be.* I applied it to everything in my life.

I wasn't entirely sure, Imposter, if I agreed with what Miguel thought about identity, about the very nature of being. I admired it, sure, as one might admire any intriguing, alien philosophy in a book. But it didn't seem to me that Miguel, powerful and authoritative and resistant to the passions and wiles of human folly as he seemed to me to be, had escaped the identity trap. It was just that he had defined his in the negative: he *was*, as determined by things he *wasn't*. He avoided roots, he rejected labels, and he ignored traditions and borders and ritual human endeavors like employment and housing. But didn't all that, in the end and despite his best efforts, aggregate to an experience, a point of view, a life?

That was bad news for me, as for a brief moment I saw an opportunity for escape in Miguel. The truth is, Imposter, I didn't *want* to be anything. I didn't want to be defined by silly notions like geography or nationality, sexuality or profession, by the rigid titles I could only ever aspire to and never fully embody.

But maybe we aren't meant to embody them, and maybe there's some freedom to be found there. Maybe there's a way to draw from both: to recognize that we are unknowable beings that exist beyond language, and to recognize that we must at times simply decide what we are and keep it moving if we are to move forward at all.

Maybe we're not so much imposters as we are actors.

Miguel and I ended up at some place on some street in some neighborhood, a two-story pastel-pink stucco house. Its connection to Miguel, who didn't live anywhere, was unknown, but we went upstairs, past other stragglers of vague nationality, where there was an exposed room without walls. We cuddled up in a hammock.

"It's sad, I think," he said, and how did I know exactly what he was referring to, Imposter? How did I know he was looking at the sky, which should have been pitch-black and dotted with stars but was instead milky and pale with lights from the resorts, the restaurants, the bars, and other human arrangements in Cabo?

"Even this, huh?" he said dolefully, and then repeated himself. "Even this."

¡Hola Papi!

*How do I let go of a relationship
that never even was?*

*Signed,
Passing Ship*

How to Spend the Night

I often found myself mirroring the way Stefan spoke, the way he didn't use contractions and added extra words like "for me" and "of course," the way many Germans spoke English. I hoped he wouldn't notice, Passing, because I couldn't get myself to stop. I thought there was something whimsical and generous about speaking that way.

I had come to Dortmund to see Stefan, a German man I'd decided I was in love with. I'd met him while studying abroad in Barcelona. We'd connected on an outdated website called Gay Romeo, which, I'd been told, gay Europeans liked to use. Oh, by the way, I lied about entirely hating my Barcelona experience earlier. Or, well, I at least overlooked some things.

Stefan had emerged from the Barcelona metro station wearing a leather jacket despite the heat, sunglasses, and black leather boots. He had wavy brown hair, and though most of him was covered up I figured he was exceptionally attractive based on the way he moved. Hot people often walk like nothing bad has ever happened to them.

He took off his sunglasses, I was proven right, and we spent the rest of the summer getting drunk in clubs, occasionally making out, and blowing each other in dark rooms. Stefan had a lightning-quick, decisive way of speaking. It wasn't that he *talked* fast—he didn't—it was that his judgments left his mouth with a haste that suggested he'd already figured the world out and was more than a little bored with it.

"Yes, it is normal," he would often say whenever I pointed something out that seemed odd to me—the way Catalans threw fireworks right down onto the street from their balconies during festivals, the way people ate dinner so late at night. "Yes, it is normal."

We parted on good terms. I went back to Oklahoma, he went to Shanghai, but we remained in touch over WhatsApp. It was about a year after I graduated college that I'd saved up enough money from my odd jobs in Oklahoma and decided to visit Stefan where he was studying advertising in Dortmund.

How did I decide I was in love with Stefan, Passing? Well, a strange memory had been cropping up. It was the day I'd met him. We'd said goodbye, and I was on the metro back to my flat. I'd missed my stop, gone two stops too far, because I'd been busy thinking about Stefan—his sauntering out of that ugly website and into my life, as he had.

Stefan had a teasing energy that got me going. "Do you like me?" he'd asked rather abruptly while we were sitting eating pizza on a cathedral step. "Are you already in love with me, John Paul? You can tell me so. I won't be mad with you."

It was easy to fall in love with a person like that, Passing. Especially later, when I had little to do in Oklahoma besides reminisce and stare at the dull ceiling of my life, looking for fantastic faces.

Stefan was in Dortmund, so I went to Dortmund. I couldn't have told you the first thing about the place. I flew into Düsseldorf and took a train to where he lived, passing by the stoic German forests that all the fairy tales and their rosy-cheeked illustrations had wandered out of.

His flat was on the top floor of a creaky walk-up. I was enchanted with this vision of his domestic life, Stefan being the kind of person who I thought had transcended the regular condition of living among pots and pans and mattresses and such. He immediately stepped into the Converse shoes I'd brought him, something he'd asked for because "they are cheaper in America," and said, "Right, we will go."

Dortmund was a college town. We ate, drank, met his friends, had sex, and quickly decided we weren't supposed to be together. There was little to elaborate on. In the end, Passing, we were entirely incompatible: his general bravado always made me feel like I was walking several paces behind him, and my occasional sullenness made him feel like he'd done something desperately wrong.

You can want to click with someone all you want. But that doesn't mean it will happen. Sometimes it even feels like it's the want itself that poisons the whole thing—the trying and the trying and the trying just ends up stretching a dynamic into unnatural shapes. I caught myself doing that with Stefan just in time. Then I met Lukas, who was entirely different; I immediately fell in love with him, rather than taking my time to decide.

And why did I love Lukas, Passing? Well, Lukas was kind and tall and curious—about the customs of people he'd never met, about the hobbies of his acquaintances, about the way everyday citizens of faraway places got around.

"We are so lucky to have the trains here in Germany, John. What do you do in Oklahoma? I want to know how you do it." He'd lean in when asking these questions. "John, I hear so often of the guns in your country. What a problem, yes? It makes me nervous for you."

Stefan was taking Lukas and me to a party in a barn near a town called Essen. We stepped out into the cold, walking out from the station into the trees. There was a line to get inside the crowded barn, and we were already drunk before we'd arrived thanks to Stefan.

I stood in stiff, awkward silence in the corner of the dance floor, observing a slice of the world that, I supposed, had been happening every week while I'd been sleeping in my room in Oklahoma. "Hallo," Lukas said in my ear from behind me. I jumped, startled, and he laughed. "Oh goodness. Oh, I'm sorry. Please, I will apologize with a drink."

He'd asked me many questions about my life before that point: about my home, about my work, about my goals. But there'd been a certain charity to those conversations, as if Lukas was just a kind person and he was this way with everyone, *anyone,* and I was no different.

But here, in the barn, I felt he was offering me something special, an energy he reserved for people he liked, actually liked. I knew it because it was an energy I'd felt before from other men, seductive and perhaps a little discourteous, the way a man will lean slightly forward and speak with more intention when he decides that he wants something, and that you have it.

We didn't even kiss that night. But, drunk and boarding the train back to Dortmund at four in the morning, I was as giddy as if he had.

The day before I left Germany, I got a WhatsApp message from Lukas. "You fly out of Düsseldorf, yes?" he said. "I live here. You can come stay the night. You leave so early."

I was so willing then to accept every torment that could possibly come with loving Lukas, from the exquisite pangs of distance to the dreary certainty that it wouldn't last. I wanted to take it all on, anything it took to have this ideal, perfect person in my life—fantasy. I wanted it.

It's only natural to feel silly for wanting something like that, as I felt when I knocked on Lukas's door. There's something a little ridiculous, Passing, about opening yourself up for such a thing, for offering the universe an opportunity to humble you.

And yet Lukas opened the door, and I found he'd set us up a card table with beers and he had soft music on. This, too, ended up feeling ridiculous, for how cliché it was, and I felt it was my duty to wade awkwardly into it, rather than jump in, lest it be exposed as a cosmic joke, as I suspected it was.

The perfect evening happened anyway. We talked about our lives, our siblings, and our bad habits. We kissed, and I told him

I would write him "a good love letter," even if, as I knew, it would come out a melodramatic mess. "Yes, I will wait for it," he said. When I finally wrote and mailed it to him, he told me, "I will cherish it."

We ended up never getting together in any formal way. The fantasy wilted almost as quickly as it had bloomed, but I didn't mind it so much. It had been the fever dream that had so intrigued me, my brief notion of loving so hard that it destroyed me, burned me alive. It could be argued I'd never actually wanted that to happen. The idea was what I liked.

I went back to Germany two years later. Stefan had messaged me asking if I'd like to visit Leipzig, where he'd moved. "You will come," he said, "and we will have a big party. I will invite Lukas and everyone from last time. Lukas is so excited to see you!"

Clearly, the idea of loving Lukas wasn't as dead as I'd thought.

I hated myself for how quickly I booked my flight, for how utterly guided I was by my sillier notions of romance. Still, I thought, not unreasonably, that there was something lucky about Stefan, and that if I continued to see him here and there he'd keep leading me to new and exciting things. He might lead me back to Lukas, for example.

We were in his car on our way to his new flat when he told me, very simply and as if it were a small thing, that Lukas wouldn't be coming after all. "Ah, yes, so strange," he said. "I told him you were coming and he seemed excited, but he has decided in the end to stay in Düsseldorf."

I used to shoot arrows out in the country with a bow. It's hard to describe how or why one knows when an arrow has been lost, before one even goes out to look for it. It's a realization that occurs the moment it's been loosed, well before it misses the target and buries itself in the grass, never to be retrieved. It was a small comfort, picturing this, in the moment Stefan told me Lukas would not be coming after all.

"Oh," was all I said. "We will have fun anyway."

"Of course!" Stefan said, like it wasn't even a question.

How silly it seems, crying over a relationship that never even happened in the first place—was never planted or watered. It simply wasn't. In mathematical terms, I'd spent barely any time with Lukas at all. I hadn't gotten to know a whole lot about him. There was never a dynamic, a familiar, reliable one, between us. We started out as just two people, and we ended that way, too. So why was I so upset?

I don't think it's "nothing" that we're mourning when it comes to our "almost relationships," Passing. I think it's fine, healthy, even, to formalize our goodbyes to mere possibilities—to things that could have happened, might have happened, the hopes and expectations and flights of fancy.

It's fine to want things. It's fine to bid them farewell.

As Stefan would tell you: it is normal.

¡Hola Papi!

How do I let myself enjoy things?

Signed,
Passive Observer

How to See a Comet
in a Room Full of Strangers

Aaron and I stood in a snaking line outside the Imperial Theatre on Broadway on a muggy September afternoon. I hadn't known there was such a fervent young fandom for *Natasha, Pierre & the Great Comet of 1812*, a musical based on *War and Peace*. But Aaron and I were surrounded on all sides by chattering teens anxiously awaiting the last performance of *Great Comet* that would ever take place here at the Imperial.

"Oh God, do you know what you've gotten yourself into?" a girl with her streaked pink hair in a loose ponytail asked, smug, I thought, but in an endearing way. She must have viewed the show itself as a boisterous, theatrical close friend of hers. She was wearing a T-shirt with the main characters on it, lines zigzagging between their portraits to illustrate the complex web of their relationships. "This is my fourth time. You're probably like, *She's crazy,* but it's really so good. I can't believe you're seeing the farewell show for your first time."

I marshaled the will to say something, anything, back. "Me neither."

The thing about that day, Observer, was that I had considered trying to kill myself the night before. Yes, I had *wanted to try* to kill myself, but when push came to shove I found I lacked the resolve. Frustrated, I'd settled on a half measure that satisfied my instinct to injury—a fistful of sleeping pills that ended up doing little more than conking me out for fifteen hours and making my bones feel like crumbly white chalk when I finally woke up. I had a blinding headache, too.

"So, like, what do you know walking into this?" the girl asked.

"It's based on *War and Peace*," I said, vaguely wondering what her fan art of the characters, which certainly existed, looked like. "It's Russian."

"They hand out pierogies sometimes," she said, all lit up. "They . . . Nope, nope, don't spoil anything, Jessica. You'll see."

My reasons for wanting to die might sound pretty dumb to you, Observer. I'd been at the Rosemont, a gay bar in Brooklyn, with some acquaintances that night and was doing what I usually did at bars: scrolling through Twitter, the website where I live. I saw I'd received a private message from an account I didn't follow.

"Why is this person coming for you?" it asked, and linked to a tweet from another person I didn't know discussing how much they hated me. "Stop putting this f*g on my timeline," the person wrote. They'd posted a screenshot of my face. Seeing my own face in enemy territory was a jarring experience—how could my own image betray me in such a way, and why was I so immediately accepting of the stranger's terms? *Yes, there really is something dumb*

about my face, I thought, *look at my big dumb ears and my big fat lips.*
I was annoyed with my face for presenting so many exploitable
openings, for being so, indeed, irritating.

The actual content of the tweet wasn't that bad. It was kind of
funny. The fact that someone out there didn't like me, probably a
jaded homosexual who lived in Brooklyn and had a podcast, was
something I could have assumed to be true without evidence.

But with a few drinks in me, it felt like a lot more than that.

Years upon years of sharing and oversharing—my thoughts,
my pictures, my words, words I didn't necessarily agree with
anymore, words I had maybe only written to meet a quota or get a
paycheck; I felt naked, like I had given too much of myself, a bad
self, away. My thoughts and ideas had been landing with people,
people who would then go on to construct their own version of
me in their minds—to this person, perhaps I was dumb; to that
person, perhaps I was inconsiderate; whatever it was, I had no
control. I had given some of the worst people alive thousands of
openings to hurt me. I was a sitting duck bobbing at the surface of
a shark tank.

I didn't want to die so much as I wanted to *not be*. I wanted to
somehow express agency over my pillaged existence. I couldn't
imagine continuing this way, being as soft and sensitive as I was
and being dragged across the rocks and bumps of life.

It wasn't about one tweet. It was about the steady, brutal hum
of life: *I exist, I exist, I exist, and I hate it here.*

Why hate it here? Well, why not? It'd been years since I'd
experienced anything dazzling in life, years since I'd looked at
something and thought, *This is why I'm here.* My everyday being

was defined by output, by desperate attempts to rise above my station and claw myself to comfort. There was no art. There was no grace. The thoughts in my head, the once-alluring shapes of things I could make and express, were immediately negotiated into word counts and pitch emails and paychecks that sometimes never came, or when they did, came very late. There were no men, no dates that left me feeling antsy, no passions or nooks or crannies to tuck myself away in.

My friends lived everywhere but where I was. What good ones I had in New York, like Aaron, lived far from me, were reclusive like me, and so I often felt alone. What I did have were critics—of my work, of my identity, of myself, and their words were some of the few that punctured through the wall of silence and reached me, because they were so sharp, so acute.

Other than that, it was as though a great, big-mouthed fish had swallowed me up, and I was in its belly, and it was so quiet, so deathly quiet, and though I was moving through life I felt nothing, and though the inside of my brain was shrieking I said nothing, and I felt in the pit of my stomach a violent desire to rebel against the nothing, to, even at great personal cost, maim the beast.

"We're moving!" the girl in front of me said. "It's all happening!"

We took our seats, and the show began as shows do: a respectful hush descends, and someone speaks with thespian authority, often heard before they are seen, and rearranges everything: we, into an audience, them, into the performers.

It quickly became clear the crowd was not here to show restraint. They'd all seen the show many times and couldn't keep themselves from rapturous applause whenever a character introduced themselves. It made it difficult to hear, but they didn't need to hear. They were following the contours of a shared, familiar experience, amplified by the finality of it all.

I did not understand the music.

I did not understand why people cried, or why they cried when they did.

I did not understand musical theater in general, really, as I so often stood in my own way of it. Seeing living, breathing actors onstage only prompted me to imagine their lives: their little apartments in Brooklyn, the drinks they'd have after this was done, the backstage with its whispered admonishments and words of encouragement and secret relationships, romantic and otherwise, tangling everything up in scandalous knots.

What little I did understand, I did not understand on the same level as the people around me, the people for whom this was a sublime experience—the last time they'd see this, the last time they'd hear this, the last time they'd be *here*. This supplied them with a secret vocabulary.

Sitting in the dark, Observer, I felt like an alien watching an utterly foreign custom. The only thing I could think to pair it all with, the only foothold I really had into it, was the night I'd had before, when I'd felt so alone and miserable and apart that I'd wanted to die. The metaphor pleased me, surrounded by the exuberance of the audience, the actors on the stage with their halos of light, and me—and who was I? I took refuge in the idea of being no one, nothing, bereft of language, excused from having to speak, temporarily exempted from the project of humanity. All I had to do was listen, and watch.

The production ebbed and flowed, hit its peaks and valleys, which were marked by the energy of the people around me; it was feverish to my blurry eyes. Russian gowns, vodka, Josh Groban (I think?), an opera, murder, infidelity, secret letters, and, hovering above it all, a comet, a light fixture threatening to illuminate and descend and end everything.

Making actual sense of what I was watching would be an uphill battle. One character could have several different names. At times, they narrated their own actions in song, in the third person. The people around me were screaming and sobbing. This was the arc of my dumb, fake little life; I understood so little about anything.

The night before, when I took the sleeping pills, I had wanted to think of something important. On the off, off chance that this act did end up killing me, I wanted to at least go out clutching some beautiful thought. But if I could have thought of something beautiful about my life, then I probably wouldn't have been in that situation in the first place, Observer. All I could think about, as my head began to swim and the edges of my vision blackened, was how small and ridiculous I was, how dutifully I had held on to my issues and problems and dramas, things that now seemed like possessions I had decided on rather than involuntarily inherited, things I acted upon out of some sense of misguided duty. I thought instead about what I would do in the likely scenario that I would go on living.

No more men, I thought.

No more body.

No more obsessing.

No more social media.

No more oversharing.

No more me.

No more, no more, no more.

I started to fall asleep.

No more. No more. No more.

I sank into the velvet cushion of nothing.

Please, no more.

Natasha, the young girl at the center of *Great Comet,* attempts to kill herself. She is caught between two loves: Andrey, her betrothed, and Anatole, the swaggering playboy. Andrey is away, dutifully fighting in the war, as one does, and it's in his absence that Natasha falls for Anatole. It's the way she loves him that captures me—she doesn't love him as some flashy, seductive object, though he appears as just that to the audience. She gives him more humanity than he has ever earned. Even from a girl hopelessly struck by him, it's an unusual humanity. She believes, with every ounce of earnestness in her heart, that he is good, that he loves her, and that they share a deep understanding with each other. Even after he is caught attempting to carry her off to Poland in the dead of night, even after he fails to come back for her, to fight for her, or to defend her in any way from the icy judgment of her peers, she defends him: "*DON'T* call him bad!"

She practically spits this line, a vicious, desperate attempt to salvage something. I don't think she's trying to defend him, Observer. Not really. She knows that's no good. I think she's trying to defend herself, to affirm, even through her utter humiliation, that some part of him was worth her time, her affection, and her love. It can't all be a waste. After all of this, after losing so much, after swallowing poison and coming out the other side, it can't mean nothing. It *has* to mean *something*.

It's here that I joined the audience in their tears, because for a brief moment, I felt I understood.

Natasha walked barefoot in a white gown, limping across the stage, frail as a fall leaf. It was all I could do to keep from weeping, because it wasn't fair. How? How was anyone supposed to stumble through this life, weak as we are, fragile as we are? I suppose we don't. Or rather, we do until we don't.

I was indistinguishable—I was so certain of it—from Jessica, from the girl in line with the pink streaks in her hair, at that point. Wherever she was in that dark crowd, our faces were probably the same. We were probably sobbing and sniffling through that sacred quiet, Natasha's proud march.

And then, it must be said, the comet.

The comet was a glorified lamp. It was perched near the ceiling, but now the play was coming to an end. Pierre had just met with Natasha, reassured her that she was a person worthy of love. Unbeknownst to them at that point, they would go on to marry and have children. Pierre stepped outside into the cold. Pierre sang about the comet, and as he did, it slowly lit up and began its long descent.

The history of stage plays is predicated on this sort of thing. In the way a roller coaster is meant to offer a controlled, but no less thrilling, brush with death, the play is meant to bring you into cathartic contact with the sublime. I must admit I'd never really experienced it, most activities involving actors and theater being entirely lost on me. But for the first time, my body and mind feeling spent, exorcised, and clean, I allowed myself to be seduced.

With my eyes, I saw a lamp. The people around me were still weeping, and I imagine they were seeing something altogether more profound than I was—the last time they'd see the comet, this comet, doing this specific thing. But I did wonder if, for once, I could give myself permission to see something the way I wanted to see it, never mind if it was fantasy, never mind if it defied my senses.

"The comet is said to portend untold horrors and the end of the world," Pierre sang as the dazzling object streaked by overhead. "But for me, the comet brings no fear. No, I gaze joyfully."

Let it be your comet, I thought. *It can be your comet, too. Let it be your comet.*

The comet continued its downward journey, glowing brighter and brighter as the music became louder; I let myself be swept away.

Maybe it turned out, Observer, that the world around me wasn't on the same page and I alone was scrambling to find it. Maybe everyone was telling their own stories, seeing *Great Comet* for the last time and thinking of their own journeys with it. And maybe trying to live life in calibration with absolutely everyone else was a naïve, harmful thing. It just couldn't be done, and so I shouldn't have tried.

When the comet at last went out and the stage went dark, an observer in the crowd wouldn't have been able to distinguish me from anyone else as I rose to my feet with them, wiping tears from my eyes, and applauded.

¡Hola Papi!

Are you even qualified to help me?

Signed,
Reader

How to Answer a Letter, Part 2

I don't know what gives people authority, Reader. I mean, a school or a certificate can give you bureaucratic authority, the kind that "matters." But that's not the kind I have to offer. I'm talking about advice, or self-help, or whatever you want to call it. What qualifies a person to tell another person what to do or how to do it?

I guess if I thought about it, I'd say it's a life lived in the general direction of correctness. People seek advice for this reason: the overwhelming notion that there are incorrect and correct choices to be made. Bad things have to happen; you learn from them and come out on the other side without letting those experiences, or their ghosts, join you and cloud your judgment.

But one thing I've learned, and I've learned it more solidly than maybe I've learned anything else, is that humans are incapable of looking at anything clearly. Even the facts of our own lives—we can only hold a few at any given time, and they shift, they slip through our fingers, they rearrange themselves into new shapes and conspire to tell a different story.

I return to the letter from a gay man I hadn't met, who lived in a place where homosexuality was illegal, and who had turned to me of all people for advice. "Can you help me?" he asked.

I wanted so badly to do just that. It frustrated me, Reader, knowing that there might be a sequence of words in me that might do some good, if I were only smart enough to string them together. They might make him feel a little better, even if they couldn't change the brutal facts of the situation: nothing I said was going to change any law in any foreign country. I couldn't be certain that telling him to express his feelings to his crush would lead to a good outcome, nor could I be certain that telling him *not* to express his feelings would lead to a safer outcome. I was powerless, as I so often have been in life.

Life!

Oh goodness, screw life. I'm getting absolutely wrecked over here. I've triangulated mine in such a way that the sex app I got addicted to shortly after coming out became my freelance employer when I accidentally became an advice columnist under the racialized moniker that white dudes liked to throw at me when they were horny. And that aspect of my life has actually been one of the shrewder, more successful things I've done. The rest has been, as you may or may not have gleaned by now, a litany of mistakes and failures.

And yet.

And yet!

I closed my laptop.

There are so many experts in the world, Reader, both real and imagined. Too many, I would say. You asked me: Are you even qualified to help me? Here is my answer: Possibly.

The truth is, I'm not that great of an advice columnist. Or at least I'm not as good at it as a lot of other people are, and there are so, so many of them. I've never quite been able to hone the voice people tend to look for in advice columns: the voice that thunders down from the heavens, delivering righteous judgment. I'm a bit too wishy-washy for that. Don't forget my column started as a parody! I can tell jokes. I am one myself, kind of.

These shortcomings aside, I have nonetheless been saddled with a responsibility, not just in my capacity as a professional advice-giver to LGBTQ people, but also as a person in a community. I have a responsibility to do my best. Erik the chlorinated Swede wasn't doing a job. He didn't have any degrees or certifications or formal qualifications. And yet, during a period of great vulnerability, he was an authority. We all have the capacity, I think, to be an authority.

But I don't answer the man's letter.

I don't attempt something I can't do.

This is wisdom, too, I think. This is helping in another way: If my voice might do more harm than good, then I am not the voice that needs to speak, even if I am in love with the sound of my own voice. There is a time for self-help and a time for self-helplessness. I think you need both to make it through life.

Identifying where I have been helpless in life has done more good for me than maybe anything else. I used to blame myself for the bad things that happened to me, and sure, I contributed. But

I can't change those things now. I can't go back and make them not happen. I can't go back and choose correctly, or in the general direction of correctness. My authority doesn't extend there. My agency doesn't extend there. I accept my helplessness there so that I might next ask myself: so what *can* I do?

Looking at things sounds like a passive activity, Reader. They manifest, and we look at them, and then we might choose to react to them. But when I look at my life, when I look at its seemingly unmovable landmarks—the pebbled wall in Cache, the plum door in Austin, the hacienda-style building of the tortilla factory—I find that looking, remembering, observing, is an active thing, it is a creative thing, and I am an agent in it.

Here is the difference between two animals: wolves howl at the moon and people make up stories about the moon. We can't live without stories. The ones we tell ourselves often end up guiding our daily lives. Maybe authority isn't real. Maybe it's just another story. And so I hope, Reader, that if nothing else, even if I can't help you, you look at your own life—the traumatic events, the men who broke your heart, the people you loved and the people you lost—and find a way, even if it's a small way, to remind yourself that you are an author.

Con mucho amor,
Papi

Acknowledgments

I would first like to thank my mom, Madre, who read books aloud to me as a kid and never asked me to switch out my artistic passions for more practical pursuits. My sister, Alex, for being my best buddy, and my dad, Padre, for letting me be myself despite all the data saying it was a bad idea.

I must also thank my Abuela, because I don't want her to haunt me, and my Abuelo, who has the patience of Job. Big thanks also go to my Auntie, with whom I said my first word. It was "moon!" Profound stuff.

As for my friends, I will thank them once I make some. A huge shoutout to my fantastic editor, Zack Knoll, who believed in this book from the jump and whose collaboration has made this project what it is today, and to my Folio agents, Annie Hwang and Erin Harris, who changed my life by representing my work.

It must be said that I couldn't have done this without the weirdly robust English program at Lawton High School, of which my mother was a part, for getting me to write and submit essays to nationwide contests and believing that I could win despite our school not having enough desks, or paper, or teachers, or ceiling tiles, or "money." A big "gracias" to Doc Freeman and Jennifer Keller on that front.

More "gracias" go to all the people who made "¡Hola Papi!," the column, happen. This includes Matt Rodriguez, who invited me to contribute in the first place, and Zach Stafford, who hit "publish" on the first "¡Hola Papi!" in 2017.

Of course, I reserve my biggest thanks to anyone who has read my work over the years. Having readers in the very first place was my biggest dream in life, and to have one, or two, or thousands, or millions has been the greatest gratification for me. So whoever you are, however you happened on my work, thank you.

A final acknowledgment goes to the Taco Bell Chihuahua. *Que descanse en paz.*

Con mucho amor,
John Paul Brammer

About Papi

JOHN PAUL BRAMMER is an author, illustrator, and columnist from rural Oklahoma currently living in Brooklyn. He runs the popular advice column "¡Hola Papi!" on Substack. His work, including essays, short fiction, and illustrations, has appeared in the *Washington Post*, *Food & Wine*, Catapult, Business Insider, and many more. This is his first book. He runs a printshop where he puts his artwork and designs at holapapishop.com. You can keep up with him on Twitter or Instagram @jpbrammer.